PLANNING FOR COLLEGES AND UNIVERSITIES: THE PRESIDENT'S GUIDE

By
Stephen D. Hogan
Harold E. Knight, III

Thornsbury Bailey & Brown

Planning for Colleges and Universities: The President's Guide

Copyright 1987 by Stephen D. Hogan and Harold E. Knight, III

All rights reserved, including the right of reproduction in whole or in part in any form.

ISBN: 0 - 945253 - 00 - 1

Library of Congress Catalogue Card Number: 87-73535

Manufactured in the United States of America

```
LIBRARY OF CONGRESS CATALOGING-IN-PUBLICATION DATA

Hogan, Stephen D., 1947-
   Planning for colleges and universities.

   Bibliography: p.
   1. Universities and colleges--United States--
Planning. 2. Universities and colleges--United States--
Administration. 3. Strategic planning. I. Knight,
Harold E., 1947-      . II. Title.
LB2341.H576  1988      378.73     87-73535
ISBN 0-945253-00-1

Published and manufactured in the United States by
      Thornsbury Bailey & Brown, Inc.
      Arlington, Virginia
```

"Would you tell me, please, which way I ought to go from here?"

"That depends a good deal on where you want to get to," said the cat.

"I don't much care where--," said Alice.

"Then it doesn't matter which way you go," said the cat.

Lewis Carroll

Previous attempts to address college and university planning usually focus on a few narrow topics, such as endowments, student recruitment, and curriculum design. Never before, though, has planning for the entire institution from the *President's* perspective been documented. This book does it.

TABLE OF CONTENTS

How To Use This Book..1

SECTION I: BACKGROUND TO PLANNING

    Why Plan? 9
    What Planning Is 13
    And What It is Not...15
    Costs of Not Planning...17
        Real Costs..17
        Opportunity Costs...19
    Who Should Plan? 21
        Trustees...22
        Administration 23
        Faculty 26
        Students..28
    Types of Planners 29
        Inactive 29
        Reactive..30
        Proactive...31
        Interactive 32

Who's in Charge? 33
    Internal Structures 35
        Trustees 35
        Professional Planners 37
        Standing Committees 39
    External Resources 41
        Consultants... 42

SECTION II: THE PLANNING PROCESS

Overview 47

Phase I: Get Organized
    Step 1 -- Organize Planning Participants 53
    Step 2 -- Adopt Planning Methodology . 57

Phase II: Establish Direction
    Step 1 -- Prepare Mission Statement 62
    Step 2 -- Define Operational Goals 71

Phase III: Collect and Analyze Data
    Step 1 -- Analyze External Situation 77
    Step 2 -- Analyze Internal Situation 81
    Step 3 -- Analyze Problems 93
    Step 4 -- Identify Priorities 99

Phase IV: Develop Strategies and Plans
    Step 1 -- Develop Operational
        Parameters..109
    Step 2 -- Design Strategies.......................117
    Step 3 -- Develop Implementation.........121

Phase V: Evaluate and Revise
Nature of Evaluations......................................133
Benefits of Evaluation.....................................135
    Step 1 -- Evaluate Planning Process.......143
    Step 2 -- Evaluate Results........................145
    Step 3 -- Revise and Update....................147
    Step 4 -- Prepare for Next Planning
        Cycle..149

SECTION III: MANAGING THE PLANNING PROCES
    Staff Meetings..154
    Correspondence..155
    Phase Reports..156
    Progress Reports...158

SECTION IV: WHY PLANS FAIL
    Why Plans Fail..161

SELECTED BIBLIOGRAPHY

APPENDIX
    The Simplex Method.......................................177
    Nominal Group Planning Model..................189

ABOUT THE AUTHORS

HOW TO USE THIS BOOK

If Herbert Kaufman, a noted authority on such things, is right, some of you are going to have a tough time keeping your colleges afloat. That, he says, is because organizations have lives of their own, quite independent of whoever happens to be in charge. Their lives are regulated by internal clocks which are not much influenced by anything mere mortals do.

This may be hard to swallow. It means that, even though you probably are a brilliant star in the academic firmament, a persuasive fund-raiser, gifted teacher, inspiring leader, recognized scholar, and all-around nice guy, you don't count for much. If your school's time is up, that's it, and there is nothing you can do about it.

Or is there? While the luck of the draw may in large measure determine which schools make it and which do not (says Kaufman), most college presidents worth their salt believe that they in fact do matter and can influence their school's future. Most are interested in excellence and how to get more of it. They are concerned with creating and sustaining thriving, prospering colleges which recognize and meet human needs. Too, they are unwilling to accept the educational status quo. Rather, they are driven by a desire to reshape the academic landscape in order to foster intellectual growth and creativity. Most presidents want more than the minimum.

Getting more, however, requires a great deal of hard work. While basic survival may be nothing more complex and demanding than a flip of the coin, real success insists on careful and thoughtful leadership. Part and parcel of that sort of leadership is sufficient attention to detail, including great regard to thorough planning. Competent planning, if anecdotal evidence is any guide, has a curious way of sojourning at those schools distinguished for their own and their alumni's achievements.

It is this kind of planning we want to help you with. We fully believe that college presidents are mostly intelligent people, frequently wise, and almost always conscientious. More important than that, we believe that you are busy, too busy in fact to spend precious time searching the vast literature for practical help with your planning needs. Doing so would be beneficial, of course, because long-time students of the subject have much to say which could help you. The problem with that, though, is that it takes too much time. It's sort of like putting up a pup tent for the first time. You can read all about the history of pup tents, the various theories on how they're constructed, and empirical studies on what researchers have discovered about them through the ages. That is all well and good. But if it's raining cats and dogs out there, you want to stick the thing up in a hurry.

How to Use this Book

Consequently, we take an approach here which dramatically speeds up the learning/application process. We use three simple approaches for getting information to you as easily as possible. First, understanding that you are busy, we abandon the usual academic format of headings, subheadings, sub-sub-headings, lengthy paragraphs encasing turgid prose, and useless footnotes. Instead, we use what we call the "bullet format" which, taking one idea per page, presents a single point in a simple declarative way. Also, we use large and sometimes bold print so you can read it easily and focus quickly on the salient points.

Second, we want to talk to you directly. As a result, we have adopted a conversational writing style which, we hope, avoids the tedium normally associated with professorial scribblings. Also, by concentrating on the needs of college presidents exclusively, we are able to keep the discussion tightly focused which we would not otherwise be able to do. However, the material we present can be useful to other college administrators and students of educational administration.

Finally, we have purposely set out to make the information here as practical as possible. This is intended to be useful, roll-up-the-sleeves, and get-the-hands-dirty information. We have tried to make everything here pragmatic and functional by culling out ideas which are not related to your job. Where

Planning for Colleges and Universities

we felt it beneficial, we have provided examples from real life as well as fiction. The latter takes the form of Buffalo Community College and Whittington College which are used to help illustrate particular points at specific junctures in the text.

To that end, after devoting brief attention to the planning background found on almost any college campus (Section I), we launch directly into our discussion of how to plan. This is presented in Section II. There are, of course, many fine schemes for producing acceptable plans. But the one we show here has always worked particularly well for us. If you follow the suggestions carefully, we feel confident that you and your staff will be able to develop and implement do-able plans tailored to your school's specific needs. They will be plans which are practical and workable and can get the job done.

Managing the planning process is the subject of Section III. People from varying, often conflicting backgrounds do not just come together and knock out a decent plan. It is not something people can do with their eyes closed. It takes long hours and set-jaw determination to produce plans the college wants to stake its future on. Controlling planners is just as hard, if not harder, as deciding what should be planned.

However conscientious you and your planners are or however good the end product is, sometimes things go sour and plans fall short. When they do, you must spend time,

How to Use this Book

energy, and money to learn how to prevent problems the next time. We offer our thoughts on the subject in Section IV.

Finally, we offer in the Appendix two of the more accessible schemes to resolve disagreement within planning circles. They will help your planners develop a consensus about critical issues before they move on to the next phase in the planning cycle.

Incidentally, now is probably as good a time as any to make an important suggestion: When planning, try to think as though you were running a business. If our experiences in education and government are any guide, leaders of too many not-for-profit institutions do not appreciate the fact that their organizations are businesses. True, they may not have stockholders and profits, but they do have products, customers, revenues, costs, cash flows, and other assorted things present in General Motors, IBM, and similar firms. Even at the risk of offending, we ask you to approach the following pages with that in mind. Planning and the planning process are much easier to grasp if you work with *all* the tools in the toolbox.

SECTION I

BACKGROUND FOR PLANNING

Background for Planning

COLLEGE AND UNIVERSITY PLANNING...

WHY?

Colleges and universities are businesses with many dimensions. They must plan in order to ensure that they remain viable and adapt to their changing environment and the market place. That is because they are:

- organizations which exist to fulfill a purpose-- without a purpose there is no need for the organization

- organizations whose goods and services must be consistent with the needs or demands of their customers

- centers of learning and science

- major employers in their areas

- a housing and living environment for their students

- communities of educators and learners.

It is the President's job to ensure the pieces of the college jigsaw puzzle fit together. He or she needs to include planning among routine management chores in order to:

- ensure that there is a specific mission or sense of direction for the institution
- provide the resources needed to achieve operational goals
- maintain and enhance the quality of the educational product
- appropriately comply with standards of excellence
- attract a qualified professional force to develop the product
- attract a continual supply of students
- maximize market competitiveness
- ensure economic viability
- challenge operations and strengthen them.

Background for Planning

Many of the problems confronting colleges and universities today can be traced to planning inertia and the confusion resulting from not having established a well thought-out course of action. Consequently **other reasons** for planning include:

- It's efficient--you can concentrate on more important things and not worry about major, last-minute glitches.

- Colleagues will be more motivated if you stick to a well thought-out plan. They need an idea of where you're leading them.

- Employee hard work, loyalty, and dedication are seldom enough to overcome disorganization, lack of direction, and a sense of helplessness.

- Coordination is easier when you know who is supposed to be doing what and when it's supposed to be done. Also, it's easier to keep all the tasks and performers straight with a plan.

- Plans have a way of sneaking into recruitment literature. It's about the best way to let potential students and parents know where the college is going. Like professors, young people want to know where you're taking them.

- Decisions throughout the year must be guided by something other than personal whim. A good plan is the framework that decision-making is based upon.

- Accreditation agencies demand evidence of planning.

- Your competition is planning.

- The pool of available students is shrinking and you're going to have to fight like crazy to get your share of it. How you intend to go about it should be outlined in the school's plans.

Background for Planning

WHAT PLANNING IS...

Planning is often a misunderstood process. In part the lack of understanding about it has retarded its use. At its best, planning is:

- above all things *your* responsibility. If you don't force the issue, nobody will and the school will flounder about without direction. The buck stops with you.

- a "change agent" that establishes the need for change when merited and the parameters by which change will occur.

- a continuum of "planning cycles" by which the lessons learned in each cycle become refined in subsequent cycles and influence their results.

- product oriented -- as the planning process is implemented, the participants must strive to associate a definable product with each segment of the plan's implementation.

- the process whereby you figure out where your school is, where you want it to go, and how you intend to get it there.

- vital because human beings cannot predict or prophesy the future with much accuracy. At the very least, planning cuts the odds of really messing up.
- a process of compromise. It represents the best the trustees, you and your staff, and faculty members have to offer.
- hard work which requires careful organization, specific activities and schedules.
- feedback which tells employees how well they are doing and how they can do better.
- a valid management function.
- the application of thought, analysis, imagination and judgment.
- an opportunity to eliminate unproductive activities and to undertake new ones.
- action based on carefully analyzed capabilities and future demands or needs.

Background for Planning

WHAT PLANNING IS NOT...

It is also useful to understand what planning is not in order to better appreciate its potential contribution. To this end planning is not:

- a cult with a "high priesthood" which makes planning incomprehensible to outsiders through the use of jargon and privileged techniques.
- magic. It involves hard work and careful direction; it does not just happen.
- simply a written plan which is relegated to a dusty bookshelf.
- a search for obvious or convenient answers.
- a short-range solution -- every decision potentially has far reaching implications into the future.
- to be feared. Many people regard planning as threatening to their security and status.

- episodic. Planning is not jumping through a hoop every five or ten years just to satisfy some state chancellor of higher education or a regional accreditation team.

- masterminding the future. The future is much too clever, complex, and unpredictable for such foolishness.

Background for Planning

THE COSTS OF NOT PLANNING...

REAL COSTS AND OPPORTUNITY COSTS

Costs of not planning are the same as not planning well. What difference does it make if planning is unprofessional, indifferent, or absent? Costs for not planning can be considered as both real and opportunity costs.

REAL COSTS OF NOT PLANNING

- Morale suffers because everyone senses that no one is in charge. No one likes working where aimlessness reigns.
- Knee-jerk responses become the rule rather than the exception.
- A style of crisis management pervades the thinking of your subordinates and trustees.

- Faculty and staff turnover become high. Nobody wants to work where it's impossible to tell where the school is heading or why.

- Lack of planning will show up in recruiting literature. Brochures which show no institutional direction and purpose are headed for candidates' dust bins.

- Financial affairs will be chaotic. Someday bankers will tire of this sort of thing and put their financial foot down. And you'll lose.

- Maintenance and other necessary expenses can be postponed only so long. Eventually the college is going to have to schedule needed expenditures if only to preserve the physical fabric of the school.

- Trustees will probably lose interest in the college. This can be devastating.

- No planning will certainly isolate you from the faculty. This is risky since they potentially can be your biggest supporters.

Background for Planning

OPPORTUNITY COSTS OF NOT PLANNING

- Prospective students will be turned off by what they don't see and hear. Potential students, especially the ones who visit campus, will sense that something is missing.

- The college will lose chances for external funding. Government agencies and private foundations want to see your plans for their monies.

- Potential benefactors likewise want to know what you're going to do with their money. If you don't show them, they'll keep it.

- Sought-after faculty members will sense, with a few well-chosen questions, that you haven't a clue as to what's going on. And they won't come.

- Ignoring planning forfeits you the chance to discover and eliminate unneeded or wasteful expenses.

- By not planning, you miss a great chance to bring faculty and staff closer together. This is especially important in smaller colleges where people want the closeness of a family.

Background for Planning

WHO SHOULD PLAN?
HOW DO YOU GET PARTICIPATION?

Once people recognize that planning is an on-going process and a required management activity, it is important to staff the work to ensure productive results. Trustees, administrators, faculty and students must participate. Collectively they usually possess all the expertise and information needed to develop a reasonable course of action for the institution and an implementation plan to manage it.

TRUSTEES...

- are ultimately responsible for the institution's operation and viability.

- must ensure that planning is pursued and that the President has the requisite resources to do so.

- should insist that your school take planning seriously. This may not be easy if key administrators or professors are fearful of losing their grip.

- must guarantee that planning is tackled professionally and that the results are realistic and feasible.

- insist that the master plan cover all phases of the school's activities, especially those with obvious interconnections.

- must see to it that sufficient time is allowed to deliberate, consult, decide on courses of action, and revise Master Plans.

- should be active and competent if they are involved with planning. Many trustees are neither; they are members for other reasons.

Background for Planning

ADMINISTRATION...

- In planning, the President is responsible for:

    -implementing the direction established by the Board

    -reporting to the Board concerning planning progress

    -stimulating the Board about planning

    -developing a reasonable and rational planning framework and process

    -assigning duties and managing the participants

    -establishing a schedule

    -reviewing individual plan components

    -integrating the components into an implementation plan

    -evaluating planning activities and modifying the planning process in subsequent cycles

    -ensuring that the plan is achieved.

- It is important that the planning process have the commitment of senior management. The President can and should provide this commitment but should not become so visible as to influence participants' creativity.

- The President must encourage participants to pursue new ideas and not simply perpetuate the status quo.

Background for Planning

Other administrators who participate in the planning process must understand the importance of their work and respond in a timely manner to their assignments. They should also:

- understand that planning is an important management function
- be given the time to make their contribution
- understand how the process will operate and the responsibilities of the participants
- be encouraged to present new ideas
- be provided sufficient feedback concerning their involvement and contribution.

The entire administration should regard "the plan" as their collective product. While compromises will be necessary (e.g., priority areas and implementation approaches), the plan provides a collective statement to the board of what needs to occur in future years.

FACULTY...

- The quality of education is directly related to the quality of the Faculty. Hence, most planning activities should relate to the quality of teachers.

- It is important to involve the faculty in the planning process. Their major contribution will be in the area of how to best implement segments of the plan. For example:

  -how to strengthen a particular school or series of courses

  -what specific resources are needed

  -how to attract more of a specific type of students

  -what the competition is in specific disciplines

  -means for ensuring professional growth

  -ways to reduce faculty attrition.

- The faculty should be encouraged to participate in discrete segments of the planning process. In larger institutions they will report to their dean. In smaller institutions they will have a closer relationship to the President.

Background for Planning

- They must take an active part in the planning process simply because they are the most significant link in the education chain.

- They should point out how they think the school can be strengthened and how its weaknesses should be eliminated. Professors may offer nothing new, but it is vital that they have the opportunity to voice their opinions. Don't cut them off.

- The faculty knows better than anyone else how to reduce faculty turnover. Ask them what they think.

- They know the competition far better than you or your trustees do. Get them to formulate plans on how to beat the competition before it beats you.

STUDENTS...

- must be included in the planning process. They are an integral part of the school's everyday life and should have voice in the way things are run.

- can contribute a great deal to a school's long-range plans if you allow them to participate. This is especially true if the school is having retention, admission, morale, or studying problems with its students.

- know the competition. After all, before they enrolled at your school, they presumably sifted through a great many catalogues and know the similarities and dissimilarities among colleges.

- need to feel like they belong and that they are important.

- like to pad their on-campus activities record with things such as across-campus committee assignments.

- will vie for planning positions in the future. This is a positive step because it means the cream of the student crop will fight for top spots.

Background for Planning

TYPES OF PLANNERS...

WHICH ARE YOU?

There are four general categories of planners: inactive, reactive, proactive and interactive. Review their characteristics and decide which applies to you.

INACTIVE:

- ride with the tide, go with the flow
- do nothing unless somebody makes you
- interested mainly in survival, not improvement
- view intervention as riskier (worse) than doing nothing
- crisis managers
- helpful if consistently moving in right direction and right speed.

REACTIVE:

- longing for the good old days
- believe yesterday was always better
- swim against the current and fight modern trends
- seen by outsiders as "muddling through"
- believe that yesterday's solution is good enough for today's problems
- personal judgment highly valued
- intuitive in nature
- work well in simple, uncluttered environments
- emphasize solutions to symptoms rather than to problems
- useful if starting to head in the wrong direction.

Background for Planning

PROACTIVE:

- believe firmly that the future will be better than the past
- try to forecast the future in order to exploit it
- want to ride with the current and participate in modern trends
- want to take advantage of the future, not control it
- more comfortable with logic, objectivity, and experimentation
- concerned with solutions to symptoms rather than with problems
- good if notice things moving in right direction but at wrong speed.

INTERACTIVE:

- want to design the future and shape it
- willing to bend the future to their own wishes
- emphasize restructuring in order to achieve objectives
- try to address root problems and not symptoms
- believe that planning is on-going, participative, integrated, and coordinated
- oftentimes highly imaginative yet risky
- frequently first phase of planning process
- unwillingness to tolerate status quo
- believe active reshaping will produce a better future.

This book is addressed to proactive and interactive planners.

ORGANIZING TO PLAN...

WHO'S IN CHARGE?

Even though the planning process has to be participatory in order to ensure success, someone has to be in charge. In larger institutions a full-time planner might direct the work. In smaller institutions the President may need to shoulder the burden.

Regardless of the structure established by the institution, some considerations must be made. The structure, for instance:

- must have the commitment of the college's senior management.

- should be functionally appropriate for the nature and volume of the planning work. Don't let the process impede the work.

- should allow for personnel assignments based on expertise, planning experience, and *a will to achieve*. Participants must be able *and* interested.

- must allow for sufficient interaction to generate new ideas and perceptions.
- should permit sufficient time to complete each task, especially for those participants with other significant responsibilities.

INTERNAL STRUCTURES

There are different internal planning structures which the college can utilize. For example:

- a long-range planning committee of the Board
- a small planning staff within the Administration
- standing committees which report to the President (or chief planner)

There are advantages and disadvantages to each structure.

Trustees on the Board's Planning Committee

Pro...

- May have the necessary authority, resources, and commitment to take charge and follow through to the end.
- Bring their own non-academic experiences and abilities to the planning process.
- Know and can persuade influential outsiders to share their expertise with college planners.

Con...

- May not have useful planning experiences.
- Probably do not have enough time to sustain a long-range planning effort.
- Often will acquiesce to demands of outspoken trustee rather than fight for their own views.
- Will begin using ad hoc meetings because scheduling formal planning sessions far in advance will prove difficult.
- Will need supporting staff to handle the paperwork.

Background for Planning

A Small Staff of Professional Planners

Pro...

- Are on campus already and can devote full time to planning.
- Relieve you of most of the burden of keeping track of what's going on in the planning sessions.
- Can easily maintain the agreed-on schedule.
- Are already known by most professors and administrators, and probably have lunch with some of them regularly.
- Probably know more about the planning process than anybody else on campus.

Con...

- May be seen by professors as "them" -- outsiders who don't really understand the nuances of the academic community.
- May begin to think of themselves as above the rest of the crowd when it comes to work schedule, perks, and opinions expressed.
- Are sometimes difficult to control because their nature is free-wheeling and creative.

- May be perceived as a threat to you if you cannot persuade them to tackle the planning problem in an acceptable way.
- Can be expensive.

Background for Planning

Standing Committees

Pro...

- Provide specific resources for a defined period of time with a singular purpose in mind.
- Can include anybody from the college community who knows something about planning or is a fast learner.
- May also include other community leaders who do not have permanent standing with the college.
- Offer a wholesome variety of opinion and level of expertise.
- Should include campus members whose planning expertise may be short, but whose loyalty, campus following, and professional stature are considerable.

Con...

- Often include somebody who doesn't seem to know anything or cannot seem to learn.
- Require detailed workplans in order to ensure that they are not derailed from their task.

Planning for Colleges and Universities

- May resent the influence of professional planners and may tend to disregard the professionals' viewpoints.

- Frequently do not understand that their role is solely to advise, never to command.

- Can be stretched too thin very quickly because of demands placed by members' routine activities.

- Can and usually do load the paperwork on full time planners (if they are around) or on administrators and their staffs.

EXTERNAL RESOURCES

There are also external resources available to assist in the planning effort. These include consultants whose expertise runs the gamut from overall planning design to data collection and program evaluation. There are also consultants who specialize in particular elements of the institutional operations such as faculty retention, finance, student enrollments and the like.

Should external planners be utilized, the following considerations will help make their participation worthwhile:

- there should be a defined scope of work or series of tasks for which external services are solicited
- the work must always generate a tangible product
- a realistic schedule is needed
- the institution should designate one individual to whom the consultants will report
- the agreed payment should be made as work segments are completed

There are advantages and disadvantages to using consultants.

Outside Consultants

Pro...

- Can offer expertise on virtually every facet of college life, including planning.
- Are comfortable with heavy workloads and quick turnaround.
- Most always are product-oriented.
- Prefer to work with the minimum of disruption to their client's activities.
- Provide necessary confidentiality in data collection, especially when asking professors, trustees and staff members for sensitive information or private opinion.
- Usually are more impartial and objective.
- Are inexpensive if they do a good job.

Con...

- Require time to learn the campus setting and personalities.
- Need detailed instructions in order to do exactly what you want them to do.

Background for Planning

- May not be able to work fast enough to get you the final plan when you want it.
- May not fully appreciate the complexities of your particular situation.
- May be expensive.

SECTION II

THE PLANNING PROCESS

THE PLANNING PROCESS...
AN OVERVIEW

The following approach to planning works; it produces results. It comprises five phases which, if carefully undertaken, will produce a master plan that will get the job done. The five are:

- Organize
- Establish the college's direction
- Collect and analyze information
- Develop action plans
- Evaluate and revise.

As a process, these five phases are sequential, as shown on the next page. Hypothetical time frames have been added to demonstrate how experience in the first cycle improves efficiency in subsequent cycles. Although our time frames are based on actual experience, your individual circumstances will affect how you schedule the planning activities.

Planning for Colleges and Universities

THE PLANNING PROCESS AND SCHEDULE

	First Cycle Schedule	**Second Cycle Schedule**
Phase I: Get Organized		
Step 1 -- Organize Planning Participants	Month 1	Month 1
Step 2 -- Adopt Planning Methodology	Month 1	Month 1
Phase II: Establish Direction		
Step 1 -- Prepare Mission Statement	Month 2	Month 1
Step 2 -- Define Operational Goals	Month 3	Month 1
Phase III: Collect and Analyze Data		
Step 1 -- Analyze External Situation	Months 4-5	Month 2
Step 2 -- Analyze Internal Situation	Months 4-5	Month 2
Step 3 -- Analyze Problems	Months 4-5	Month 2
Step 4 -- Identify Priorities	Month 5	Month 2
Phase IV: Develop Strategies and Plans		
Step 1 -- Develop Operational Parameters	Month 6	Month 2
Step 2 -- Design Strategies	Month 6	Month 3
Step 3 -- Develop Implementation Plan	Month 6	Month 3
Phase V: Evaluate and Revise		
Step 1 -- Evaluate Planning Process	Month 7	Month 3
Step 2 -- Evaluate Results	Months 7-12	Month 11
Step 3 -- Revise and Update	Month 12	Month 12
Step 4 -- Prepare for Next Planning Cycle	Month 12	Month 12

The Planning Process

The five phases must be followed sequentially in the order given which is really only common sense. What good, for example, would it do to start developing actions plans if you haven't even bothered to figure out where the college is going? If you don't follow the correct sequence, the whole planning effort may be thrown out of kilter.

You will notice as you move forward with your own planning efforts that you will want to change some of the things you've already decided on. For instance, as you start analyzing information, you may discover that the facts of college life do not support the direction your planning group listed early on. If they don't, go back and change them. Do not proceed any further until you do. Otherwise you will lose control of both the planning process and the final plan.

Also, one further remark is probably in order here: As is obvious, not everybody involved in planning will agree on what should be done. All parts of planning are subject to disagreement. Some people, for instance, will want to aim the college in one direction while others will want to aim it in another. Too, even if planners agree on a direction, they probably will not agree on how to get there. Some may plead for more demanding curriculum and others will argue for stricter admission standards. If those are the only choices and you cannot have both, which one should your planners pick?

Helping out are the materials in the Appendix. Of the numerous methods available for resolving group disagreements, we have chosen two which have always produced results for us, the Nominal Group Planning Model and the Simplex Method. Both offer fairly straightforward approaches for reaching group consensus. They can be used throughout the entire planning cycle, including setting the college's mission, its strategic targets, its actionable plans, and its evaluation plans.

The difference between successful plans and unsuccessful plans is that the former get implemented and the latter do not. The implementation activities must be carefully developed and requires a strong senior management involvement. Suggested management techniques are described later in Section III.

* * * *

The remainder of this section describes each planning phase, its activities, products, and supporting information. As each phase is discussed it is presented in the context of the entire process.

Here we go with Phase I...

The Planning Process

THE PLANNING PROCESS

Phase I: Get Organized	Work Products
Step 1 -- Organize Planning Participants	planning group convened planning memo planning methodology timetable
Step 2 -- Adopt Planning Methodology	

Phase II: Establish Direction
Step 1 -- Prepare Mission Statement
Step 2 -- Define Operational Goals
Phase III: Collect and Analyze Data
Step 1 -- Analyze External Situation
Step 2 -- Analyze Internal Situation
Step 3 -- Analyze Problems
Step 4 -- Identify Priorities
Phase IV: Develop Strategies and Plans
Step 1 -- Develop Operational Parameters
Step 2 -- Design Strategies
Step 3 -- Develop Implementation Plan
Phase V: Evaluate and Revise
Step 1 -- Evaluate Planning Process
Step 2 -- Evaluate Results
Step 3 -- Revise and Update
Step 4 -- Prepare for Next Planning Cycle

The Planning Process

PLANNING PHASE I...

GET ORGANIZED!

Close attention should be paid to organizing properly. If this phase is overlooked, chaos will result. There are two major activities in Phase I: organize the planning participants and develop the planning methodology.

STEP 1: ORGANIZE PLANNING PARTICIPANTS

Planning cannot be successful without the institutional commitment to it. The following will strengthen that commitment:

- Organize the planning participants before the first meeting and make sure everyone understands who will be in charge. This person may be you, a dean, the president of the faculty, a respected professor, the chairman of the trustees, or an outside consultant.

- Appoint a small planning group, usually no more than three or four persons. A larger number will be difficult to control and likely to be slow in getting any work done.

- Planning participants should include people who have proven themselves especially able on past assignments. Get people who are committed and will produce results. Do not chose people as a reward for previous work, as an effort to get them out of the way, or as a means to punish them with a heavy committee load.

- Distribute a brief statement to the entire college community which endorses planning, describes in general terms the process which the planning group will follow, and announces who will serve [see next page for a sample].

- At the first meeting, remind all participants of the process of planning as outlined here. It may be necessary to modify it a little to accommodate the particular needs of your school. Do not be reluctant to tinker with the specifics, but do not abandon the general format. If you do, you may become bogged down later on.

The Planning Process

EXAMPLE OF PLANNING ANNOUNCEMENT

TO: Board of Trustees
                         Administration
                         Faculty Members
FROM: President G. Washington
SUBJECT: College Planning

    I am pleased to announce that we will soon adopt a new approach to college-wide planning. It should enable us to consider our mission, strategic targets, and operating activities more thoroughly than ever before. The results should help to improve the school's focus, operations, and ability to serve our students.

    The new planning process has five phases:
- organizing the participants and methodology
- establishing our mission and overall direction
- collecting and analyzing pertinent information
- designing alternatives
- evaluating our accomplishments.

    Professor Betsy Jones has agreed to serve as chairman of the planning committee. Also serving will be Dean Billy Bob Smith, Professor Luigi O'Toole, and Francesca d'Rimini of the Board.

    They will need your help and will want to talk to all of you. Please give them your cooperation. I know they will greatly appreciate it. Try to answer their questions as candidly as possible because only in that way can they get a handle on what you really think. And please be assured that all remarks will remain private and confidential.

    I believe this is a worthwhile undertaking and hope each of you join with me in welcoming this opportunity to improve our academic program and our community service. If you have a specific interest which you would like to share with the committee, please contact Professor Jones. I am sure she will be most happy to work out a meeting schedule.

The Planning Process

STEP 2: ADOPT PLANNING METHODOLOGY

The next order of business will be to adopt a planning methodology and schedule. The process contained in this Guide has proven successful, but it may be necessary to adapt it a little to meet individual institutional circumstances.

The methodology provides the framework within which all other planning activities take place. It is important to utilize a methodology that:

- is straightforward and uncomplicated
- all the key participants will understand including the conceptual design, purpose and products
- requires a logically programmed sequence of activities that are technically sound
- is reasonably inexpensive to execute
- will generate information needed to make logical decisions.

Again, this Guide assumes that the planning methodology you end up with will be similar to what we have here. Consequently, the remainder of the Guide will focus on implementing that methodology.

And now for Phase II. . .

THE PLANNING PROCESS

Phase I: Get Organized
Step 1 -- Organize Planning Participants
Step 2 -- Adopt Planning Methodology

Phase II: Establish Direction   **Work Products**
Step 1 -- Prepare Mission   mission statement
           Statement   goal statements
Step 2 -- Define Operational Goals

Phase III: Collect and Analyze Data
Step 1 -- Analyze External Situation
Step 2 -- Analyze Internal Situation
Step 3 -- Analyze Problems
Step 4 -- Identify Priorities

Phase IV: Develop Strategies and Plans
Step 1 -- Develop Operational Parameters
Step 2 -- Design Strategies
Step 3 -- Develop Implementation Plan

Phase V: Evaluate and Revise
Step 1 -- Evaluate Planning Process
Step 2 -- Evaluate Results
Step 3 -- Revise and Update
Step 4 -- Prepare for Next Planning Cycle

The Planning Process

PLANNING PHASE II...

ESTABLISH DIRECTION

Most colleges know the general directions they want to go. Usually they are implicit and unwritten, have evolved over time, and have been handed down by senior administrators, long-time professors, staff, or even the Board of Trustees. Often they have their origins in some immediate crisis or very obvious need.

But specific directions are sometimes reactive rather than proactive and as such do not lend themselves to comprehensive planning. More than anything else, these directions comprise what the school does not do rather than what it does. Most people do not think about why they do things the way they do them. Instead, they know only why they do not do them.

STEP 1: PREPARE MISSION STATEMENT

The first step in establishing direction is to develop a mission statement. Some institutions may already have one which probably details:

- commitment to higher education
- provision of quality education
- and other philosophical ideas.

Existing mission statements tend to be directly related to the past environment or believed purpose of the institution. But a mission statement should:

- consider the changing environment of the institution
- provide for changes in the educational market place
- challenge existing organization and operational practices
- include institutional values
- be an honest and realistic assessment of the institution's purpose.

The Planning Process

If the mission statement is not realistically crafted, all that follows in the planning process will be unrealistic as well. Time and money and opportunities will be lost. Hence, the mission statement should be developed along the following lines:

- It should state unequivocally why the school exists and why parents should pay to send their children there. This requires a great deal of thought and introspection.

- Plain ordinary English should be used. It is a death wish to use fancy-dress academic language because it almost always has the effect of confusing everybody, including your paying customers.

- Include a brief discussion about the kind of education your school tries to offer: classic liberal arts, vocational, technical, work-oriented, fine arts, heavily scientific/ mathematical, highly structured, minimally structured with mostly electives, or self-designed.

- Comment on the type of student you want to attract. If your college accepts everybody, say so. If not, say which sort of student you want in simple words.

- Be student-oriented. Pay close attention to their needs and make sure you market the school well in your mission statement.

- The statement should be accepted by the college community. Trustees must understand and approve it, as must all administrators, teachers, and support staff. A simple declaration of intent helps set the course for the college and is something everybody needs to see.

The Planning Process

Now consider the following examples of actual mission statements:

> **Augsburg College:** "...provide high quality educational opportunities which are based in the liberal arts and shaped by the faith and values of the Christian church and by the context of a great metropolitan center."

> **DePauw University:** "...to seek truth and educate minds. To foster the love of learning and the increase of knowledge, and to recognize and support intellectual and creative excellence. To enlarge capacities for clear, thorough, and independent thought. To understand and appreciate cultural and scientific achievements. To encourage serious reflection on the moral and religious aspects of experience. To respect and sustain the freedom of inquiry and speech. To demonstrate integrity and honesty, courage and compassion...."

College of St. Teresa: "Assist students in acquiring intellectual and personal habits needed to develop and sustain a sense of responsibility and self-direction. Create opportunities for the development and the execution of leadership skills useful in contemporary life. Provide opportunities to participate in a campus community composed of persons who have come together in pursuit of truth. Maintain an environment which enables students to grow as persons in all aspects of life and to show their talents in the service of others. Develop a campus community characterized by a commitment to Judaeo-Christian moral values as exemplified in the life and teachings of Jesus Christ."

University of Virginia: ". . .to enrich the mind by stimulating and sustaining a spirit of free inquiry directed to understanding the nature of the universe and the role of mankind in it. Activities designed to quicken, discipline, and enlarge the intellectual and creative capacities, as well as the aesthetic and ethical awareness, of the University and to record, preserve, and disseminate the results of intellectual discovery and creative endeavor serve this purpose. In fulfilling it, the University plans the highest priority on achieving eminence as a center of higher learning."

The Planning Process

These examples raise questions that should be addressed in designing your mission statement:

- While they are grand-sounding statements, who are they for: administrators, professors, researchers, groundskeepers, benefactors, students, parents?

- Would peers use these as grounds for granting or denying tenure?

- Would trustees use these as measures of your performance?

- Do they say anything helpful to potential students and their parents who are struggling to differentiate among schools?

- Would students not particularly interested in having their intellectual and creative capacities quickened, disciplined, and enlarged, but only in getting a sheepskin, be kicked out of school?

- Do these statements overdo it by promising experiences serious and conscientious young scholars can only provide for themselves?

TWO FICTIONAL EXAMPLES

Perhaps it would be helpful now to hypothesize a couple of different scenarios and speculate on what the mission statement of each should say. Consider these two fictional settings:

Buffalo Community College (BCC) is a rapidly growing, state-supported two-year school with three campuses scattered about the greater Buffalo metropolitan area. Enrollment currently is 4,000 FTE and should increase to 5,000 FTE when the fourth campus in nearby Columbia is opened year after next. Most entering students succeed in getting an AA degree, even though most take longer than two years because they must work. The most popular majors are retailing and accounting, with over 40 percent of all students.

BCC's mission statement might appear as follows: "The purpose of Buffalo Community College is four-fold:

> 1) to offer the chance for a beginning college education to all students, regardless of social, economic, or academic background;

> 2) to lead students toward vocational skills which they can use for the remainder of their working lives;

The Planning Process

3) to encourage students to take charge of and design their own academic programs based upon their individual needs; and

4) to provide the Buffalo area with a pool of solid talent which will serve to brighten the future of the entire region."

Whittington College (WC) is a small liberal arts, Presbyterian four-year college located in rural Indiana. Enrollment has held steady for the last three years at 600 FTE. All students are full-time and all single students live on campus. Even though the college does not encourage it, many students work part-time in area businesses. WC is quite expensive--a full year's tuition, room, and board runs to $12,000. Like most private schools, it works diligently to search out financial aid for its students. Income from the school's endowment fund has declined for four years straight because of the depressed condition of its major holding, Indiana farmland. The most popular majors are economics and history.

WC's mission statement might be: "Whittington College strives to offer each student a broad-based liberal education, rooted firmly in the classic disciplines of arts, humanities, sciences, and religion. Students with such an education are better prepared for thoughtful, purposeful, and mature lives. The course of study, which is quite rigorous, is designed to create citizens of the world."

* * * *

We will return to these two fictional examples from time to time to illustrate specific points.

The Planning Process

STEP 2: DEFINE OPERATIONAL GOALS

The next step in setting the direction of the planning process is to develop a series of operational goals. These can be characterized as statements that:

- further define the mission statement
- address areas of the college in which financial and human resources will be focused
- help to compartmentalize the focus of the planning process and yet permit subsequent aggregation into the final plan.

It may be difficult initially to be specific in developing operational goals prior to assessing the college situation which occurs in Phase III. However, they can be modified after the situation analysis is completed.

Planning for Colleges and Universities

Buffalo Community College

Increase the faculty/student ratio to 25:1 in order to make better use of both faculty and classroom space

Improve academic standards over a five-year period so that area four-year colleges will accept more BCC students without probation

Try to improve the college's image in the local community.

Whittington College

Earn at least twelve percent on endowment funds

Develop imaginative new schemes for helping graduates find employment

Reduce the faculty/student ratio from its present 10:1 to 8:1 within five years.

And Phase III next...

THE PLANNING PROCESS

Phase I: Get Organized
Step 1 -- Organize Planning Participants
Step 2 -- Adopt Planning Methodology

Phase II: Establish Direction
Step 1 -- Prepare Mission Statement
Step 2 -- Define Operational Goals

Phase III: Collect and Analyze Data	Work Products
Step 1 -- Analyze External Situation	external analysis
Step 2 -- Analyze Internal Situation	internal analysis problem analysis
Step 3 -- Analyze Problems	priorities analysis

Phase IV: Develop Strategies and Plans
Step 1 -- Develop Operational Parameters
Step 2 -- Design Strategies
Step 3 -- Develop Implementation Plan

Phase V: Evaluate and Revise
Step 1 -- Evaluate Planning Process
Step 2 -- Evaluate Results
Step 3 -- Revise and Update
Step 4 -- Prepare for Next Planning Cycle

PLANNING PHASE III...
COLLECT AND ANALYZE DATA

It is difficult to predict exactly how much effort will be required to collect, process, and analyze the data needed to support the planning process. That is because initial efforts will likely generate additional data requirements and these will need to be accommodated as they arise. Also, because all campus situations are different, various kinds of data may be needed and these needs are impossible to catalogue in detail.

It is possible, though, to organize the process into four major data collection and analysis activities:

- external analysis
- internal analysis
   - -collegiate personality profile
   - -management profile
   - -operational profile
   - -student profile

- problem analysis
- priority analysis

Existing data should be used wherever possible. If absolutely necessary, though, additional information can be gathered with limited special studies. However, bear in mind that these take valuable time and money. Consequently, before beginning any data collection activity, ask yourself the question, "How much information do we need to make a decision?" Then try to get by with the minimum amount.

The Planning Process

STEP 1: ANALYZE EXTERNAL SITUATION

The environment outside the campus community in some respects shapes everything which happens on the inside. All planning must incorporate an analysis of the external environment because it governs if and how your college will be able to continue as it has and change in the future. There are literally dozens of different ways to consider the external world. However, all of them wind up gathering and analyzing data on demographics, economics, and the competition.

Demographics

- Indicate the available pool of college-bound high school seniors and the non-traditional student as well.

- Reveal trends which will heavily influence a college's long-range plans. These plans must allow for shifts in focus and interest (e.g., the declining interest in sciences, mathematics, and foreign languages).

- Identify how many potential students in your particular market satisfy your school's academic requirements.

- Graduate school continues to grow in popularity and may have an influence on your school's programs. How?
- Does the trend toward more married students and/or students living with one another interfere with meeting your school's long-term objectives?

Economics

- Of students available, how many can afford to attend your college full time and part time?
- Are ample financial aids available for any and/or all students?
- Has your college enrollment followed the business cycle and, if so, what is the forecast for the economy for the next four years?
- Are government grants and student loans scheduled to continue at present levels?
- How economically prosperous is your main marketing region and what are you and your school going to do if things get substantially better or substantially worse?

Competition

- Are other colleges in your marketing area taking away potential students from your school by using tactics and programs which you have not?

- Have high school counselors become lukewarm in selling your school or are they really trying to market you?

- Are your tuition, room and board, and fees price competitive?

- Do potential students perceive that they would receive good value for their money at your school versus other schools?

- Define your school's market and describe in detail how other schools are tapping into it. In some respects this must be done by considering the college's mission statement and major goals.

Buffalo Community College

BCC's market is entirely local and no other state-supported junior college operates in the area. Also, the various private traditional and business colleges cannot compete with either the diversity of course offerings or the low price. The trade-off, of course, is BCC's large class size which other local schools are now beginning to take advantage of. On the whole, though, the college is fast moving into a monopoly position in its particular market.

The Planning Process

STEP 2: ANALYZE INTERNAL SITUATION

It is important to analyze how serviceable are the college's mission statement and its declared goals. To that end, it is necessary to characterize the internal operations of the institution in a way which will allow members of the planning committee to evaluate both mission and goals. Probably the best way to do this is by analyzing the college's present situation by profiling its personality, management, operations, and students.

These profiles must be in writing. It is no good for planners to agree that everybody already knows all about the school's personality and its administration, operations, and students. That may be true. But it is crucial that planners' views and perceptions be committed to paper. This will accomplish two things. On the one hand, it will force members to address an issue which they too often take for granted. And on the other, it allows planners to discuss the various perceptions and to separate fact from fiction.

Collegiate Personality Profile

This is the sum total of campus culture. Part of it is found in formal documents, like policy and operating manuals. Most of it, though, is informal and largely constitutes "the way we do things around here". To develop the profile, a series of interviews will be needed. The following suggestions should help:

- Individual personalities are strong influences on a college's personality: colorful, petty, scholarly, busy, stupid, motivated, frustrated, happy, or lazy.

- Tradition plays a powerful role. Active alumni, level of research, leadership quality, student involvement, teaching emphasis, formal dances, intramural activities, vocal faculty senate, and others work together to shape the college's individuality.

- Expected responses also enter in: the finance vice president who always says no, the dean who can never be pinned down, professors who always (never) find time for students, maintenance's prompt reaction to problems, or the library's inability to collect fines.

- Rewards and punishments indicate how much risk-taking is wanted. Many schools do not tolerate any novel approaches and severely reprimand those individuals who try something different. Others welcome newness and reward well if it succeeds.

- Decision-making processes show who really has the power. Many presidents grant almost exclusive franchise to their deans to handle internal affairs, while others demand personal review of everything which goes on. The same is often true with deans, vice presidents, department chairmen, and operating managers.

- Internal politics and on-campus rivalries influence the college personality: ambitious versus laid-back professors, up-to-date researchers versus out-of-touch colleagues, energetic trustees versus catatonic ones, deans who want to boot you out and take over.

- Informal communication channels--the grapevine--are frequently a large influence on a school's personality and should be considered when analyzing the present situation.

Whittington College

The faculty senate has a tradition of active involvement in the affairs of the college. This stems primarily from most professors' views that all phases of Whittington's curriculum are heavily interdependent. Hence, it is virtually unthinkable for one discipline to undertake action on its own without consultation with and approval of the entire faculty.

As at many colleges, Whittington's senior professors tend to be out-of-date professionally and leave to their junior colleagues the chore of writing for publication. This situation influences how academic matters are considered on campus. Most old-timers resist change if it interferes with their way of working and newcomers are frustrated because they are consistently outvoted in the senate.

Finally, the Vice President for Finance is seen by almost everybody on campus as something of an idiot. Students complain that he harasses them constantly about parking tickets and activities fees. Professors have given up trying to make sense out of his unique payroll accounting system. And the Trustees don't even bother trying to understand what he's doing--they only hope that the annual audit gives a clean check.

Management Profile

This profile characterizes the management philosophy and capabilities. Conducting this portion of the internal analysis poses interesting questions that will affect the planning effort:

- What are top administrators' philosophies of management and their respective:

    -roles and purposes?

    -levels of personal involvement?

    -responsibilities for the school and its paying customers?

    -roles as change-agents or reactors?

    -relationships of personal interests and school's interests?

- What are the leadership abilities of the college in terms of their:

    -use of internal and external politics to the school's advantage?

    -understanding of the marketplace and ability to market the school well?

    -recruitment of top people and effective use of them?

    -provision of overall direction?

- What are the operating abilities of the college in:

    -upgrading the level of fiscal sophistication?

    -viewing the value of self-studies and accreditation visits?

    -acting to improve organizational weaknesses?

    -insisting that operating data be timely and useful?

    -looking beyond personal friendships to doing what is right for the school?

The Planning Process

Operations Profile

Operational data will be needed in areas such as:

- service and program descriptions
    - purpose for each operating unit
    - number of students served
    - budgets
    - self-generated funding
    - grants and subsidies
    - gifts
    - availability of services and programs.
- personnel descriptions
    - number of full-time, part-time, and volunteer
    - academic specialty or professional expertise
    - educational background
    - personal data (e.g., age, gender)
    - period of employment and/or service
    - number of different classroom preparations
    - number of classes

-faculty/administration turnover

  -recruiting sources

  -morale.
- support service descriptions

  -motor pool

  -internal communications

  -contract services

  -honorary associations

  -student activities

  -library quality

  -financial aid

  -career planning and counselling

  -book store quality.

The Planning Process

Buffalo Community College
Personnel Information:
Full-time employees — 422
Part-time employees — <u>106</u>
528

Teaching employees
    Full-time — 201
    Part-time — <u>45</u>
246

Average Salary
    Full-time employees — $19,540
    Full-time teachers — 25,100

Education
    Full-time teachers
        B.S. — 12
        M.S. — 147
        Ph.D. — 142
    Part-time teachers
        B.S. — 21
        M.S. — 75
        Ph.D. — 10

Student Profile

The student profile provides insights about your customers and should address:

- admission information
    - recruited or voluntary application
    - ACT or SAT scores for each class
    - ratio of accepted to enrolled.
- academic information
    - proportion of new students needing remedial classwork
    - proportion on academic scholarship
    - grade point averages for each class
    - grade point averages for non-graduating students who do not return
    - proportion of students eligible who return
    - number graduated each year
    - scores on exit comprehension exam
    - proportion of each class on academic probation.

The Planning Process

- personal
  - -average age
  - -proportion of each class requiring/receiving financial aid
  - -proportion of graduating class going to graduate school
  - -study habits
  - -morale
  - -demographic data.

The student profile can help you develop customer patterns and improves your product line and marketing skills.

Whittington College
Academic Information
Cumulative GPA

Freshmen	2.21
Sophomores	2.46
Juniors	2.70
Seniors	<u>2.89</u>
All	2.49

Students on Dean's List

Freshmen	3
Sophomores	5
Juniors	8
Seniors	<u>7</u>
All	23

Proportion on Academic Scholarship

Freshmen	18
Sophomores	21
Juniors	10
Seniors	<u>10</u>
All	15

The Planning Process

STEP 3: ANALYZE PROBLEMS

It is likely that the principal force encouraging colleges to begin planning is a series of problems. They should be analyzed to determine their:

- nature
- extent
- origins
- interrelationships
- impact on operations
- subsidiary organizational effects
- possible solutions
- management responses.

The primary source of data for problem analysis probably will be focused interviews with key personnel. The interviewing teams must be particularly mindful of the need to maintain respondent confidentiality during the reporting of the responses. This will help encourage frank and earnest discussions and minimize subsequent surprises. The following suggestions should facilitate your problem analysis:

- Problems, or discrepancies between reality and the ideal, must be addressed in a logical, coherent, and thorough way.

- The nature of the problem must be analyzed: why is it a problem and for whom?

- How extensive is the problem and will it go away if you leave it alone?

- Some problems may seem to fall out of the sky but seldom really do. It is important to a thorough understanding of the situation to discover why the trouble cropped up now and where it came from.

- Can this particular problem be self-contained or will it spread to other areas? This is especially important for smaller schools where everybody knows everything and secrets do not exist.

The Planning Process

- A severe or even minor problem may have unfortunate rippling effects on other parts of the school. Try to figure out in advance what might happen to other units if the problem is not contained quickly. Then take steps to head it off.

- Do not attach blame. The planning effort should be directed at solving pressing problems.

- Consider the variety of management responses which are available. Sketch out possible near-term and long-term solutions. Then attempt to dovetail them into an optimal solution. Scale your potential response to the size of the problem.

- Insist, even when discussing known or perceived problems, that absolute confidentiality and secrecy be maintained.

- Make sure your planners exhaust all possible problem areas so that neither they nor you will be surprised later on by something everybody should have foreseen.

The following are examples of problems you may uncover:

- Should that old unused dormitory be closed down permanently or should funds be raised to convert it into future office space?

- The regional accreditation agency insists that your school upgrade its library collection before it grants re-accreditation. But doing so would require an expansion in the library building and there simply isn't any room.

- Two students get into a violent fist fight which ends when neighbors summon the police. The story is front-page news the next morning.

- Nobody takes Professor Thomas' math classes any more because she's a terrible teacher. She is tenured, though, and you can't figure out what to do with her.

- Employees have enjoyed handsome returns to their aggregated retirement fund courtesy of a great bull market. Some of them, though, worry that it's time to bail out. Others are not so sure.

- Faculty turnover averages over 20 percent a year. It seems like professors are either brand new, fresh out of graduate school and not very good teachers yet; or else they have been there forever and out-of-date. No middle-term profs are around any more.

The Planning Process

- The English faculty and students loathe the department chairman who can't be fired because he has strong personal ties with influential trustees and community benefactors.

- There are never enough commuter parking spaces and students are beginning to block neighborhood driveways. Neighbors have threatened legal action and the police have started towing away vehicles.

- Junior professors want to restructure the salary/rank system put in place by their senior colleagues. But the old-timers don't want to share the wealth.

Buffalo Community College

The parking problem is getting worse and no one on campus knows what to do about it yet. But something must be done quickly. Homeowners in the neighborhoods surrounding the mid-town campus have recently gained a court injunction to prevent BCC from acquiring any more property to convert into parking spaces. The Fire Marshall has already stated publicly that student commuters and the resulting congestion constitute a severe hazard to fire protection. And the municipal transit authority wants a guaranteed minimum of 2,000 rides a day before it will initiate special bus services for BCC commuters.

STEP 4: IDENTIFY PRIORITIES

Priorities are like beauty--they are in the eyes of the beholder. Everyone has his or her own perception which may or may not be consistent with the overall operations of the school. Regardless of any differences of opinion, though, priorities must be established [see Appendix] for the mission statement, goals, problems, and solutions. Analyzing priorities should consider:

- What is important in a school's life depends upon individual tastes and perceptions.

- Some coherent, organized scheme must be installed for ranking problems and solutions in some order acceptable to the whole college community.

- Unless differences in opinion are resolved systematically and amicably, there is very little chance that important problems will be solved at minimal institutional cost. Sometimes they won't be solved at all.

- Without some device to give everyone a chance to be heard, the most vocal, powerful, senior, or intimidating individuals will dominate the planning discussion. This could be disastrous.

Examples of conflicting priority areas that may arise in your college include:

- Buying peace with old-fashioned trustees by agreeing to invest endowment funds in Certificates of Deposit, despite the fact that letting respected investment managers handle the funds could substantially raise the school's endowment income without increasing risk.

- Using scarce funds to hire a needed intramural sports director instead of a go-getter development officer.

- Letting the president of the faculty prowl through the internal audit report even though you'd rather not. It's probably better to let him satisfy his curiosity than make a big stink over it. Also, if you're lucky, he won't understand a word of it.

- Creating a new standing faculty committee to review tenure/promotion applications instead of giving too much power to the already standing personnel committee.

- Buying WATS time for the admissions staff instead of leasing another van for the theater faculty.

The Planning Process

- Letting the quality of the expensive business faculty slide and using the extra money to improve dramatically the quality of the humanities faculty.

- Insisting that no more typewriters be purchased and that all business equipment monies be spent on personal computers.

- Agreeing to let the college turn your on-campus home into more offices in exchange for an increase in your housing allowance so that you can buy something you really want instead.

- Making the choice to eliminate the Language Department because nobody much cares any more and using the money instead to put in a new septic system.

- Ensuring that the recently retired chaplain is replaced even though most students on campus are heathens.

- Allowing department chairmen to purchase supplies from off-campus sources if they can get them cheaper than in the college bookstore.

USE OF PRIMARY DATA

Sometimes secondary sources of information will not be adequate. If not, you must go directly to primary sources, such as professors, students, trustees, community leaders, and patrons. The following considerations should prove helpful to you:

- Interviewees must be selected with great care. Never allow candidates to be chosen who merely have an axe to grind. You need a balance of viewpoints.

- Make sure the planners determine their specific data needs in advance of the interviews to be sure everyone asks the same questions and can then compare notes with each other.

- It is *vital* that information gathered during personal interviews be treated confidentially. Absolutely no leaks should be tolerated. If they occur, find out who's doing it and get rid of the person. This rule of confidentiality cannot be over-emphasized. If it is compromised in the least, your planning team will lose its greatest strength--credibility--and the quality of its work will be severely reduced.

The Planning Process

- Try to take time to have the survey instrument tested in advance. This is especially true if the questions are involved and/or sensitive.
- Make sure the information survey is carried out according to the rules and on schedule.
- Be careful not to overdo this interviewing business. It can be expensive and time-consuming.

THE PLANNING PROCESS

Phase I: Get Organized
Step 1 -- Organize Planning Participants
Step 2 -- Adopt Planning Methodology

Phase II: Establish Direction
Step 1 -- Prepare Mission Statement
Step 2 -- Define Operational Goals

Phase III: Collect and Analyze Data
Step 1 -- Analyze External Situation
Step 2 -- Analyze Internal Situation
Step 3 -- Analyze Problems
Step 4 -- Identify Priorities

Phase IV: Develop Strategies	Work Products and Plans
Step 1 -- Develop Operational Parameters	operational criteria strategies to solve problems
Step 2 -- Design Strategies	ideas for strategy implementation
Step 3 -- Develop Implementation Plan	implementation plan

Phase V: Evaluate and Revise
Step 1 -- Evaluate Planning Process
Step 2 -- Evaluate Results
Step 3 -- Revise and Update
Step 4 -- Prepare for Next Planning Cycle

The Planning Process

PLANNING PHASE IV...
                DEVELOP STRATEGIES AND PLANS

The term "strategies" is an elusive one and often connotes different things to different people. In this Guide, it means a series of organized activities designed to achieve a predetermined accomplishment. Sometimes this will entail designing corrective action for a specific problem area. Oftentimes strategies will prescribe a new course of action for the college to follow.

Designing action strategies is the real core of the planning process. It is where all the work of the planners finally comes together. The work now becomes detailed, technical, and action-oriented. Planners can no longer afford to be general and philosophical. They have already established the direction they wish to go. Now they must figure out how to get there. Three distinct steps are now required: establish parameters, formulate strategies, and develop implementation (and contingency) plans.

Remember that we said planning was a continual process? This quickly will become evident when you realize that one action plan often becomes refined over time and generates additional and complementary action plans.

The Planning Process

STEP 1: DEVELOP OPERATIONAL PARAMETERS

The first activity after analyzing the data is to set forth operational parameters. By undertaking this activity, the strategic responses of the plan can be tailored specifically to address the institution's mission and goals. The criteria comprising the operational parameters will originate from the following areas:

- environment (internal and external)
- market
- financing.

The criteria will guide the development of strategic responses and implementation strategies.

Environmental Criteria

Each institution's internal and external environmental pressures are different. These are the elements the institution must consider in designing any strategy. Typically they include:

- information obtained from:

    -situational analysis including collegiate personality, management, operational and student profiles

    -problem analysis

    -priority analysis

- recognition of existing affiliations (e.g., state, community, and religious) which will affect new strategies and their operation

- scheduling requirements (e.g., filling certain faculty positions for accreditation, preparing for new student enrollments, program frequencies, etc.)

- special funding interests (e.g., dedicated endowments and associated requirements)

- image of the institution in the immediate community and among the alumni

The Planning Process

- special interest groups within the institution (e.g., individual faculty desires, administration/trustee interests, etc.)
- internal/external politics
- contractual obligations (e.g., plant maintenance, building programs, etc.)

Market Criteria

The institution's market can be viewed from many perspectives. At the minimum, the criteria should address:

- who purchases the college's services (e.g., students, parents, alumni, benefactors, grant authorities, etc.)
- whether the present market will be strengthened
- whether new markets are needed
- internal perceptions about acceptable marketing techniques
- internal/external competition for resources and purchasers
- market trends and fluctuations.

The Planning Process

> **Whittington College**
> - Sixty percent of students come from within 150 miles (including Indianapolis).
> - There is a definite trend toward more urban students than rural students.
> - Unless the farm economy improves substantially, the college may have to step up its efforts to recruit students from farther away.
> - Some high school counselors have expressed reservations about recommending the college because of its liberal arts emphasis. High school seniors may fear being unable to find employment after they graduate from Whtitington.

Marketing criteria are important for establishing strategies because they influence how to finance new programs and facilities and expand existing ones.

Financing Criteria

Financial criteria should be designed to recognize parameters of future strategic activities. Specifically, they should address the institution's perspectives of:

- short-term vs. long-term profitability
- how much risk is acceptable
- capital availability
- overall financial position
- program contributions to profit
- departmental/programmatic budgeting and accounting
- establishing cost center accounting procedures.

The Planning Process

> **Buffalo Community College**
>
> - Fluctuating heating oil prices have played havoc with cash flow estimates. This past winter, $50,000 had to be siphoned from the library's book budget to pay for heat.
>
> - The Metropolitan Education Council has increased BCC's allocation for capital spending to $3.5 million from $3.0 million.
>
> - Estimated cost for insurance premiums was $25,000 too low. Next year premiums are slated to rise another $40,000.
>
> - All budget and cost accounting data will be fully computerized by the end of the academic year. No more manual systems will exist.

Again, operational parameters are important because they establish the boundaries within which the desired strategies will be developed. If the criteria are ignored, the results could be disastrous. But the criteria must represent an institutional consensus--they cannot be dictated. Achieving consensus will be more difficult for some criteria than others. The group decision making techniques contained in the Appendix can help.

The Planning Process

STEP 2: DESIGN STRATEGIES

After operational parameters are finalized, the various strategies can be designed. They will address future implementation activities, such as:

- expanding the market
- increasing enrollments
- improving buildings and grounds
- attracting more endowment gifts
- strengthening specific academic areas
- improving operating procedures.

Each strategy should:
- be consistent with the mission statement
- relate to a specific goal
- be consistent with applicable operational criteria
- be internally sound
- consider the relationship with other strategies.

Planning for Colleges and Universities

On the following page is a handy format for developing strategies. It will be helpful in addressing the most important elements necessary in actually designing new strategies. By completing the form for each new strategy, planners have an opportunity to summarize all of the preceding work and focus it on each strategy. This provides a manageable amount of information to be used in designing implementation plans.

The Planning Process

STRATEGY DEVELOPMENT FORM

Strategy Title:

Relevant Goal:

Applicable Operational Parameters:

Strategy Development Activities:

Resource Requirements:

Organizational Responsibility:

Relationship to Other Strategies:

Implementation Considerations:

Potential Problems:

The Planning Process

STEP 3: DEVELOP IMPLEMENTATION PLAN

The implementation plan should include specific action plans as well as contingency plans to ensure that each strategy becomes operational. These plans are the essence of the planning process. All the prior meetings, discussions, arguments, data collection, and analytical work culminate in the plans. The following suggestions will be helpful to you in developing your implementation plan.

Action Plans

- They must be consistent with the college's mission statement. This is why it is so important to have a statement which actually means something.

- They should relate to a specific goal. Because many strategic targets are sometimes quite involved, it may be necessary to have a series of action plans.

- They should be consistent with appropriate management, operating, and financial parameters established earlier.

- They must be considered in terms of other plans already undertaken or soon to be.

- Indicate in detail how strategic targets will be reached. This cannot be overstated. It is imperative that your planners state in unequivocal, simple, straight-forward, comprehensible language exactly what the action plan is supposed to accomplish.

- You should also devise a logical, well-researched schedule for completing the plan. Since other strategies and plans depend on it, the timetable you develop is serious business.

The Planning Process

- Resources should be allocated for completing the plan. Too often planners neglect this simple item if only because it is usually fairly obvious. Nevertheless, planners should go to the trouble of writing down, in detail, what will be required to get the job done.

- Identify individuals who will be given specific tasks to do. Assignments must be thought out well in advance and should take into consideration individuals' personalities, their other commitments, their willingness, and their abilities.

- You ought to prepare a discussion of potential problems which might short-circuit either actual implementation or the timetable.

- Make sure that you prepare a calendar of when each element of the plan should be finished. This can take the form of a PERT chart or Gantt chart. This will save a lot of frustration and headache, not to mention expense, if you run into trouble and have to make changes in the schedule.

- They should be designed so performance can be measured. Otherwise, you may wind up with only fuzzy, meaningless results.

Whittington College

- Commission the college's accounting firm to evaluate the feasibility of leasing versus buying nearby apartment buildings to use as married student housing.

- Decide if the water-damaged pipe organ in the leaky chapel is worth repairing.

- Run hiring announcements in the *Chronicle* for new history, literature, and mathematics professors in order to reach the goal of 8:1 faculty/student ratio.

The Planning Process

Contingency Plans

A few comments are in order here:

- Contingency plans are necessary because few plans ever work out exactly as you'd like.

- It is not much trouble to revise departmental or divisional plans because they don't involve large-scale, long-term philosophical issues.

- Significant changes in broad, college-wide objectives take a long time and are hard to achieve. In effect, the college must replan from scratch.

- Simple contingency plans should be considered and attached to implementation plans. It is fairly easy to postulate alternative scenarios when adopting long-range plans. Those alternatives can be the starting point for sketchy plans to be fleshed out if necessary.

- Alternative scenarios must be quite different from each other and from the one used in planners' forecasts. They should be plausible, realistic, and possible, even if unlikely.

- They force planners to become more informed and knowledgeable about the future of their college. These people then can be used as valuable resources in the future.

- They reflect well on the college's management. Administrators who neglect contingency planning, even of the sketchiest sort, are putting all their future eggs in a single basket. Not smart.

- Implementation plans should contain specific triggers for activating contingency plans.

Buffalo Community College

- When the Columbia campus is opened, enrollment balloons to 5,500 which is 500 above target.

- The price of heating oil rises much more than expected, shooting from $0.80 a gallon to $1.15.

- Buffalo's Metropolitan Education Council cuts its annual subsidy from $1,200 FTE to $900.

- The trustees fire the president.

When all the strategies and contingency plans are aggregated, they become the implementation component of the master plan. While details of each program and strategy are contained in their respective documentation, the implementation plan serves as a point at which they are summarized and readied for activating.

The Planning Process

On the following page is a suggested Gantt-chart format to assist you in developing your implementation plan. By developing the chart, you can begin to monitor the implementation activities.

On to Phase V...

IMPLEMENTATION PLAN [GANTT CHART]

ACTIVITIES	IMPLEMENTATION SCHEDULE	Assigned Person	Comments
1.			
2.			
3.			
4.			
5.			
6.			
7.			
8.			
9.			

WORK PRODUCTS:

The Planning Process

THE PLANNING PROCESS

Phase I: Get Organized
Step 1 -- Organize Planning Participants
Step 2 -- Adopt Planning Methodology
Phase II: Establish Direction
Step 1 -- Prepare Mission Statement
Step 2 -- Define Operational Goals
Phase III: Collect and Analyze Data
Step 1 -- Analyze External Situation
Step 2 -- Analyze Internal Situation
Step 3 -- Analyze Problems
Step 4 -- Identify Priorities
Phase IV: Develop Strategies and Plans
Step 1 -- Develop Operational Parameters
Step 2 -- Design Strategies
Step 3 -- Develop Implementation Plan

Phase V: Evaluate and Revise	Work Products
Step 1 -- Evaluate Planning Process	evaluation design process evaluation outcome evaluation
Step 2 -- Evaluate Results	preliminary revisions and updates
Step 3 -- Revise and Update	
Step 4 -- Prepare for Next Planning Cycle	

The Planning Process

PLANNING PHASE V..
EVALUATE AND REVISE

Evaluation of plans and their implementation are not cutomary in higher education. They should be. Turning a blind eye to actual versus planned results is not wise because, in the long run, it compromises the vitality of the school. Evaluation of enacted plans is critical because it forces the planning process to an orderly conclusion. You and the trustees must ensure that proper evaluation takes place. It is also important because the conclusion of one cycle of planning is the beginning of the next. If one planning cycle never ends, it's logical to suppose the next can never begin.

The Planning Process

NATURE OF EVALUATIONS

The term "evaluation" often connotes a less than positive meaning to many people. They associate evaluations with punitive actions. This is unfortunate because evaluations can be a very good management tool. To successfully evaluate anything, the following elements must exist:

- Evaluation must focus on how to reach the targets set forward earlier. They must address how to improve a college's product or its services.

- Evaluation should be done in measurable terms if possible. Planners should take great care in designing plans so that their success or failure can be easily determined. Usually that means evaluating with numbers.

- If numerical evaluation is not feasible, be sure to devise an alternative which everyone accepts as politically neutral. If you don't, you will assuredly polarize the college community.

- Data used for evaluation purposes must be valid. This is especially true if there is disagreement among planners over what the results actually say.

- Any evaluation must follow the procedure outlined and be accepted by planners during the planning design stage. This assures everybody that evaluations were carried out as impartially as possible.

- Every effort must be made to strip away personalities from the evaluation process. This will be hard, especially if strong personalities are present, but must be done. That is why agreement must be reached in advance over what evaluation procedures will be followed.

BENEFITS OF EVALUATION

Evaluation should not be considered a punitive process. Rather, it is a means to improve operations which can benefit the four main groups involved in planning: trustees, administrators, faculty, and students.

Benefits to Trustees...

- Evaluation supplements and sometimes sanctifies inputs from administrators, some of whom are trying to guide organizations too large and unwieldy for one person to handle.

- It provides overall feedback on how well the planning effort is working.

- It indicates if plans approved by trustees are actually reaching their objectives. This is good politics because trustees like learning if something they approved did as intended.

- It gives trustees an opportunity to revise important policies and programs based upon evaluation results.

- It adds an element of the dynamic to the operation. This is important because trustees appreciate being associated with progress.

- It improves communication between the administration and the board.

- Also, it helps trustees understand what's going on. This can help them build up the college in the local community.

- Evaluation grants a wonderful opportunity to reward good performance.

The Planning Process

Benefits to Administrators...

- Evaluation gives positive accountability to the board and the local community.

- It shows the faculty and staff that planning is taken seriously. This cannot be over-emphasized because everybody, especially faculty members, want to feel that their views are being heard.

- It indicates the commitment of the college to a continuing planning effort.

- It provides operating and financial feedback on the efficacy of both planning and the plans themselves.

- Evaluation helps future planning for staffing, bank borrowing, tuition collection, and many other resource allocation issues.

- It helps to minimize surprises.

- It helps ensure coordination among involved parties and guides them toward better coordination in the future.

- It enhances the overall image of the college because word gets around that you and your planners know what you're doing. This is critical for "honeying up" to potential benefactors: they like to support winners.

- It forces the integration of planning cycles to minimize administrative confusion.

- In the long run, it always makes for easier and more pleasant work.

Benefits to Faculty...

- Evaluation gives them a chance to express their opinions on the efforts of the planning committee. By giving everybody an opportunity to contribute, you automatically disarm a lot of inappropriate criticism.

- It helps faculty members understand what's going on and perhaps gives them a better appreciation of the intricacies of the college's operations.

- It helps them feel like they belong.

- It allows them the chance to make suggestions which you and your planners may never have thought of. It is unwise not to take advantage of such an intelligent and frequently imaginative resource.

- It begins to develop an on-campus awareness for what planning can do and how to go about it. It also helps to build confidence.

- Evaluation makes future planning easier because it starts developing a cadre of people who know how to plan. Next year, planning efforts will move more smoothly and faster because experienced people will be available to offer advice and assistance.

- It may contribute to more effective research efforts. Some faculty members are not well organized and do not use their research time efficiently. By seeing the benefits of advanced planning, perhaps they can begin to apply the same planning techniques to their own work.

Benefits to Students...

- Evaluation provides planners with a unique opportunity to bounce ideas off the college's customers. If the paying clients think ideas or plans are good, they'll probably tell you so. This is valuable information because it suggests future progress for the college.

- It can encourage an enormous variety of serious suggestions, imaginative ideas, and creative counsel which administrators should heed or at least consider.

- It provides them with a sense of belonging. This is especially important in smaller schools.

- The evaluation process gives them a feeling of where the college is going and how it intends to get there. If students approve, they can be influential marketers for the school in the future.

- They have a vested interest in seeing that the school thrives because their degrees become more valuable in society's eyes.

The Planning Process

STEP 1: EVALUATE THE PLANNING PROCESS

The plan can be evaluated from two perspectives: the process followed in developing it and the results achieved.

- A step-by-step review of the process which produced the master plan should be undertaken. The reason for doing this is to find out if any glitches in the planning results were caused by a short-circuit in the planning process.

- The review should determine if planners followed their own declared process for developing plans. Also, it should determine if they patterned their process after an acceptable formula.

- All documents must be made available for review. The purpose is not to scold planners for their mistakes, if any. Rather, it is to learn what exactly took place and to learn from the results. This is a necessary part of the planning cycle and no one should be offended to have his work reviewed.

- Who should evaluate the planning process? It depends mainly on how well the plans work out. If they do as expected, the people who produced the plans are probably able to provide a decent review. If plans do not work out, perhaps it would be better if someone else did the review. That way, there can be no criticism of the evaluation process.

- This evaluation demands a thorough examination of timetables and schedules in order to determine if they were realistic.

- Committee minutes, if detailed, may provide a wealth of information about the planning process. If planners chose not to have detailed minutes, the reviewer(s) may wish to meet privately with each planner and ask if the process of planning was followed.

The Planning Process

STEP 2: EVALUATE RESULTS

The following thoughts will help you with your evaluation activities:

- Sometimes actionable and even strategic plans generate a lot of activity, much paperwork, and very little else. Their purpose is still to achieve the college's mission.

- Results-evaluation provides a chance to assess if desired results match up with actual results.

- It is important that desired and actual results be stated in comparable and measurable terms, e.g., a 10 percent increase in enrollment for the fall semester, at least a 15 percent average annual return on endowment funds, or automating the monthly insurance paperwork on the computer.

- Periodic review gives administrators and trustees a feel for how well implementation is progressing. Such progress reports are valuable for maintaining control of operations.

- Each phase of a strategic or action plan must be analyzed to see if it contributed to or interfered with reaching a plan's objective. This is to ensure that the organization behaves in a fashion consistent with its mission and strategic direction.

The Planning Process

STEP 3: REVISE AND UPDATE

It is important to revise and update the plan and planning process for the following reasons:

- No plan is perfect because it deals with the future. Consequently, it will contain mistakes, miscalculations, bad assumptions, and poor execution. This should not be seen as a problem. Rather, it should be viewed as an opportunity to learn and correct.

- All information taken from on-going evaluations should be used to alter implementation activities if it appears that things are going awry. There is absolutely no sense in sticking with a particular program if it is wandering badly from what you want.

- Information from planning reviews can be used to improve plans during the next cycle and make them work easier.

Planning for Colleges and Universities

- Revision provides a good chance to alter timetables for specific activities in future planning cycles. This is especially important for schools just beginning to plan in an organized way and still feeling their way about.

- Planners will learn quickly that they may need to devote more effort to certain aspects of the planning process than they originally thought. Too, they will learn that more or less resources are required to get the job done which will help their thinking during the next cycle.

- Updating of not-yet fully implemented plans is necessary in order to fix anything that may have gone wrong. This is simple information feedback and should be used to adjust or fine-tune on-going activities.

- It is probably a good idea to examine previous revisions and updates to see if they worked out as desired. If they did, great! If they didn't, try to figure out why and avoid the same mistakes again.

The Planning Process

STEP 4: PREPARE FOR NEXT PLANNING CYCLE

With the completion of this step, you have concluded one full planning cycle. This experience and the lessons you have learned can be well employed when you continue the process in the next cycle. Remember, planning is a continuous process which, frankly, should become easier with each application. Some suggestions to make it easier still are:

- Convene a meeting of the major participants and review previous planning activities and how they can be strengthened.

- Review primary and secondary data collection activities and find ways to make them more efficient.

- Schedule Phase I activities for the next planning cycle.

- Introduce new participants into the process in order to provide the school with a future pool of expertise and talent.

- Review the minutes and notes of the planning group to discover any problems that you personally may be able to solve when the next cycle begins.

- And above all, Get Started!

Here comes Phase I . . .again.

SECTION III

MANAGING THE PLANNING PROCESS

MANAGING THE PLANNING PROCESS...
A FEW USEFUL TECHNIQUES

To this point, the discussion of planning has focused on what planning is, how the process can be implemented and how the college's planning efforts can be organized. Recall that planning is hard work, both for planners and implementors. It is also hard work for presidents because they must make sure that the planning process, the plans themselves, and the implementation are well managed. You or someone else must work diligently to ensure that control is exercised in order to keep the effort from straying from its purpose.

Standard procedures can be helpful to you and your planners to make sure everything progresses on schedule. These relate to staff meetings, correspondence, phase reports, and progress reports. But, management activities should be kept as simple as possible and consistent with routine operations so they do not interfere with the real activities of the college. Nobody wants to create a monster.

STAFF MEETINGS

The planning process entails the coordination of many people through the different phases of work. Periodic staff meetings are:

- necessary to coordinate activities of everyone involved in the planning process
- valuable for keeping abreast of the status of both planning and implementation activities
- appropriate for considering any problems encountered and how they should be resolved
- vital for getting a consensus on major points, such as the college's mission, its strategic targets, and its priorities
- probably the best way for revising parts of the planning methodology which don't work
- good for assigning people to specific chores and group discussion can most always avoid hard feelings or conflicts

Minutes should be taken at each meeting and sent to each member. How detailed the information is must be decided by the group and your management requirements.

Managing the Planning Process

CORRESPONDENCE

The planning process will generate a variety of correspondence:

- announcements
- policy statements
- requests for information
- memoranda assigning work
- progress reports.

These should be retained in a central file and referred to as needed.

PHASE REPORTS

Each phase and subordinate activities of the planning process should be documented. The planning leader must track who is doing what, when it is completed vs. when anticipated, and resource requirements. Additionally, comments about the activities and their interrelationship should also be maintained. The Summary Activities Schedule on the following page can be useful for providing an overall perspective of the work in each phase.

Managing the Planning Process

SUMMARY ACTIVITIES SCHEDULE

Planning Phase: _____
Phase Leader: _____

Activites	Expected Completion Date	Actual Completion Date	Personnel Assigned	Comments and Interaction Points

PROGRESS REPORTING

An important means for reviewing the progress of the institution's planning efforts is through monthly progress reporting. Each month a brief progress report should be prepared by those personnel responsible for identified activities. These reports should not be lengthy, but should adequately describe the activities during the previous month, future planned activities, and problems encountered and how they were resolved. The progress reports should be distributed to the appropriate personnel. A copy should be filed along with the Phase Reports. During the year, these reports can be reviewed and discussed at staff meetings and during the evaluation work in Phase V.

SECTION IV

WHY PLANS FAIL

WHY PLANS FAIL

Sometimes plans do not work. When dealing with millions of dollars of physical plant, hundreds or thousands of students, future funding uncertainties, great faculty mobility, and changing educational standards, plans can fail to measure up. It is not that planners devise bad plans on purpose; it just works out that way sometimes.

But failure in planning can be minimized. The best means is through practice. With each planning cycle the error potential decreases because you become more experienced and comfortable with planning. The participants understand better what is expected of them. The policy base established in the first phase of the first year becomes refined. Your data collection and analysis activities become more reliable. Your evaluation skills sharpen. Meanwhile, elements of your plan may fail or be less successful than you desire. Often the reasons for this can be identified and controlled. Some of the more common reasons are:

- tolerating unresolved issues which can have disruptive effects on the future of the college

- planner and/or administrator uncertainty about what to do

- timidity and inability or unwillingness to see and take risk
- lack of real commitment to planning
- inability to move quickly on emerging issues
- unwillingness to delegate planning responsibilities
- not using the same planning process twice to ensure continuity
- confusing planning studies with plans
- making decisions with no clear-cut purpose in mind
- poor communication among planners, trustees, administrators, and other key personnel on campus
- underestimating the importance of the key assumptions used to produce plans
- treating strategic targets as plans--they're not--they tell you where you want to go; plans tell you how to get there
- wrong people doing the wrong job--abilities, desires, convenience, and willingness all must be considered when matching people with jobs

- basing plans on past experiences rather than future expectations--history does repeat itself, but not in much detail
- poor diagnosis by planners
- mutually antagonistic priorities, such as increasing faculty/student ratio while trying to attract more qualified faculty members
- planning periods which do not dovetail into each other
- forgetting to make performance measurable
- using the wrong measures of performance
- not tying together plans and objectives from various segments of the college
- using unclear, imprecise, or trendy language in important plans
- ill-conceived priorities
- not allowing for resistance to change
- being unaware that personal goals and organizational goals may conflict.

SELECTED BIBLIOGRAPHY

SELECTED BIBLIOGRAPHY

Bergquist, William and Jack Armstrong. *Planning Effectively for Educational Quality*. San Francisco: Jossey-Bass Publishers, 1986.

Blum, Henrik L. *Planning for Health: Generics for the Eighties*. New York: Human Science Press, 1981.

Carroll, James, Bernadette L. Skobjak, and Mark Emmert. "Revising a College's Planning System: Translating Theory into Practice." *Planning for Higher Education* (Fall, 1984), pp. 23-28.

Coleman, Donald G. "Strategic Planning: A Case Study in University Change Through Value Added." *Planning & Changing* (Fall, 1985), pp. 177-188.

Cope, Robert G. "A Conceptual Model to Encompass the Strategic Planning Concept: Introducing a New Paradigm." *Planning for Higher Education* (Spring, 1985), pp. 13-20.

Delaney, Robert and Robert Howell. *How to Prepare an Effective Business Plan*. New York: AMACOM, 1986.

Delbecq, A. L. and A. H. Van de Ven. "A Group Process Model for Problem Identification and Program Planning," *Journal of Applied Behavioral Science* (July, 1971), pp. 361-376.

---------. "The Nominal Group as a Research Instrument for Exploratory Health Studies," *American Journal of Public Health* (March, 1971), pp. 337-342.

Delbecq, A. L., A. H. Van de Ven, and D. H. Gustafson. *Group Techniques for Planning Programs*. Glenview, Illinois: Scott, Foresman and Co., 1975.

Fenske, Robert H. (ed.). *Using Goals in Research and Planning*. San Francisco: Jossey-Bass, 1978.

Gardner, James R., Robert Rachlin, and Allen Sweeney (eds.). *Handbook of Strategic Planning*. New York: Wiley and Sons, 1986.

Hammermesh, Richard G. *Making Strategy Work: How Senior Managers Produce Results*. New York: John Wiley and Sons, 1986.

Heaton, C. P. (ed.). *Management by Objectives in Higher Education*. Durham, North Carolina: National Laboratory for Higher Education, 1975.

Bibliography

Heller, Jack F. *Increasing Faculty and Administrative Effectiveness*. San Francisco: Jossey-Bass, 1982.

Holloway, Clark (ed.). *Strategic Planning*. Chicago: Nelson-Hall, 1986.

Ingram, Richard T. (ed.). *Handbook of College and University Trusteeship*. San Francisco: Jossey-Bass, 1980.

Jedamus, Paul and Marvin Peterson (eds.). *Improving Academic Performance*. San Francisco: Jossey-Bass, 1980.

Kaufman, Herbert. *Time, Chance and Organizations: Natural Selection in a Perilous Environment*. Chatham, New Jersey: Chatham House Publishers, 1985.

Klee, Albert J. "Let DARE Make Your Solid Waste Decisions," *The American City* (Feb., 1970), pp. 85-99.

Koontz, Harold. "Making Strategic Planning Work," *Business Horizons* (April, 1976), pp. 37-47.

Lilly, Edward R. "The American College President: The Changing Roles." *Planning & Changing* (Spring, 1987), pp. 3-15.

Lotto, Linda S. and David L. Clark. "Understanding Planning in Educational Organizations." *Planning & Changing* (Spring, 1986), pp. 9-18.

McCorkle, Chester O., Jr. and Sandra Orr Archibald. *Management and Leadership in Higher Education*. San Francisco: Jossey-Bass, 1982.

Merson, John and Robert Qualls. *Strategic Planning for Colleges and Universities*. San Antonio, Texas: Trinity University Press, 1979.

Miller, Richard I. *The Assessment of College Performance*. San Francisco: Jossey-Bass, 1979.

Montfort, E. Riggs, III. "Strategic Management Impotence: An Advisory to Chief Executive Officers." *Planning Review* (January, 1984), pp. 12-14.

Mouritsen, Maren M. "The University Mission Statement: A Tool for the University Curriculum, Institutional Effectiveness, & Change." *New Directions for Higher Education* (Fall, 1986), pp. 45-52.

Bibliography

Peters, Thomas J. and Robert H. Waterman, Jr. *In Search of Excellence: Lessons from America's Best-Run Companies*. New York: Harper & Row, 1982.

Peterson, Marvin W. "Continuity, Challenge and Change: An Organizational Perspective on Planning." *Planning for Higher Education*, Vol. 14, No. 3 (1986), pp. 6-15.

Reinharth, L., H. J. Shapiro, and E. A. Kallman. *The Practice of Planning*. New York: Van Nostrand Reinhold Co., 1981.

Richardson, Richard C., Jr. and Don E. Gardner. "Designing a Cost Effective Planning Process." *Planning for Higher Education* (Winter, 1985), pp. 10-13.

Scott, Cynthia Luna. "Launching Successful Planning Efforts." *Planning for Higher Education*, Vol. 14, No. 2 (1986), pp. 26-29.

"The Simplex Method." Unpublished monograph. Washington, D.C.: Arthur Young and Co., 1976.

Ulschak, F. L., L. Nathanson, and P. G. Gillan. *Small Group Problem Solving*. Reading, Mass.: Addison-Wesley, 1981.

VanGrundy, Arthur B. *Techniques of Structured Problem Solving*. New York: Van Nostrand Reinhold Co., 1981.

------. *Managing Group Creativity.* New York: AMACOM, 1984.

Vaughn, George B. *The Community College Presidency.* New York: Macmillan Publishing Co., 1980.

Webster, William E. "Operationalizing the Planning Process in Schools: A New Look." *Planning & Changing* (Summer, 1985), pp. 82-87.

Wolotkiewicz, Rita J. *College Administrator's Handbook.* Boston: Allyn and Bacon, 1980.

APPENDIX

GROUP PROCESS DECISION MAKING TECHNIQUES

APPENDIX

There are many practical ways to structure how planning groups make their decisions. Almost all of them have been around a while and most, despite their theoretical beginnings, have evolved into strictly functional, deliver-the-goods approaches. If their rules are followed carefully, planners will be able to get their work done in good order and on time.

We have chosen to describe only two methods here, the Simplex Method and the Nominal Group Planning Model. This is because, out of the two or three dozen currently available, these two have worked consistently well for us. That is not to say that other approaches are not valid and do not produce acceptable results. They probably do. But we're going to stick with what we know. If you would like a sampling of what else is out there, check the bibliography for ideas, especially Van-Grundy.

Appendix

The Simplex Method

Planners in disagreement over important issues can reach a consensus by using the Simplex Method.[1] It requires them to respond to a series of direct questions on the problems they disagree on. Answers they give are scored and the results averaged. The largest average indicates the issue which should be given top priority. Other issues follow in order. The same procedure applies for developing a solution consensus, too.

Since the Simplex Method is fairly straightforward, it is probably best to describe it by using a hypothetical example. Suppose, for instance, that planners disagree over which of three problems facing the college should receive first attention. The problems are: declining enrollment, low faculty morale, and a poor image in the community.

Step 1: By whatever means they chose, planners should develop a list of questions for each problem. There is no reason to expect the same questions to apply to all issues. Consequently, for the case in point, there should be three different lists of questions, one list for each issue. Questions should have five possible answers, answer 1 indicating a minor problem and answer 5 a major one. These questions should be approved by the entire decision-making group. While a unanimous vote is

---

[1] Modified from an unpublished monograph, Arthur Young and Co., Washington, D.C.: 1976.

certainly desirable, a simple majority may have to do. Any major disagreements must be negotiated away before anybody begins answering. The questionnaire can be as long or as short as planners wish. However, a very large number of questions probably will be redundant and a pain in the neck.

Step 2: The questionnaire should then be distributed so that each planner may answer in private or at least where no one can try to influence his choices. When everyone has answered, the questionnaires will be collected and tabulated. Hypothetical results are shown in Exhibits 1-3.

Appendix

Exhibit 1
Problem: Declining Enrollment

Planner	A	B	C
1. **Declining enrollment affects:**	3	3	4

   1. very few on-campus people
   2. a minority of them
   3. half of them
   4. a majority
   5. everybody

2. **Declining enrollment's effect on the college's long-term viability:**	2	2	3

   1. negligible
   2. very slight
   3. moderate
   4. significant
   5. very detrimental

3. **Left unattended, this problem:**	1	2	4

   1. will go away
   2. is likely to go away
   3. will stay the same
   4. is unlikely to go away
   5. will not go away

4. **The extent of the short-term damage caused by declining enrollments is:**	2	2	4

   1. negligible
   2. mild
   3. appreciable
   4. serious
   5. total

5. **Declining enrollment's effect on faculty morale is:**	3	2	3

   1. none
   2. imperceptible
   3. noticeable
   4. serious
   5. devastating

Exhibit 2
Problem: Low Faculty Morale

Planner	A	B	C
1. Over the next five years, faculty morale will:	3	2	5
1. get much better			
2. get better			
3. stay the same			
4. get worse			
5. get much worse			
2. If left unattended, low faculty morale:	3	3	4
1. will go away			
2. is likely to go away			
3. will stay the same			
4. is unlikely to go away			
5. will not go away			
3. Time lost because of low faculty morale is:	2	1	3
1. none			
2. little			
3. appreciable			
4. serious			
5. very serious			
4. Low faculty morale's effect on declining enrollment is:	1	2	4
1. none			
2. slight			
3. noticeable			
4. appreciable			
5. great			

Appendix

Exhibit 3
Problem: Poor Image in the Community

	Planner	A	B	C
1.	How serious is the college's poor image in the community? 1. not serious at all 2. somewhat serious 3. serious 4. grave 5. a death wish	3	2	3
2.	If left unattended, the college's image in the community will: 1. get much better 2. get better 3. stay the same 4. get worse 5. get much worse	3	4	4
3.	The attitude of community leaders toward the college is: 1. very interested 2. interested 3. complacent 4. indifferent 5. antagonistic	4	5	5
4.	For this problem, it is probably best for the college to: 1. do nothing 2. do little 3. meet community leaders partway 4. meet them halfway 5. aggressively attack the problem	4	4	5
5.	To solve this problem, the college currently has on-campus programs which are: 1. more than adequate 2. adequate 3. barely adequate 4. inadequate 5. hopeless	3	3	5

Planning for Colleges and Universities

Step 3: Tabulating these numerical results requires averaging the scores for each question, totaling the averages, and dividing the total by the number of questions. The resulting grand averages will range from a low of 1.00 to a high of 5.00.

Issue	Planner	A	B	C	Total	Average
Enrollment Decline						
Question	1	3	3	4	10	3.33
	2	2	2	3	7	2.33
	3	1	2	4	7	2.33
	4	2	2	4	7	2.67
	5	3	8	3	8	2.67
					Total	13.00
Low Morale						
Question	1	3	2	5	10	3.33
	2	3	3	4	10	3.33
	3	2	1	2	6	2.00
	4	1	2	4	7	2.33
					Total	11.00
Poor Image						
Question	1	3	2	3	8	2.67
	2	3	4	4	11	3.67
	3	4	5	5	14	4.67
	4	4	4	5	13	4.33
	5	3	3	5	11	3.67
					Total	19.00

	Total of Averages	Grand Average
Enrollment Decline	13.00	2.60
Low Morale	11.00	2.75
Poor Image	19.00	3.80

Appendix

Step 4: These grand averages indicate that Poor Image is the problem which planners believe should be addressed first, followed by low faculty morale and declining enrollment. However, a word of caution is in order. Experienced planners should establish a cut-off point below which problems are not addressed at all. For example, a grand average of less than 2.5 might indicate that the problem is really not so pressing as people originally thought. Planners may wish to postpone dealing with it until another time. Naturally, this scheme is arbitrary and should serve only as guidance, not as final decision.

Step 5: With Poor Image identified as the premier problem facing the college, it is now necessary to consider how the problem should be solved. Planners should repeat the process just described, substituting "solutions" for "problems". To continue the illustration, suppose that planners believe there are four different solutions to the school's image problem. They are: hire a top-notch public relations firm to fix the problem, hire renowned visiting professors, make admissions standards much tougher, and beautify the campus. A separate list of questions for each solution must be developed and answered by each planner. Results are shown in Exhibits 4-7.

Exhibit 4
Solution: Public Relations Firm

	Planner	A	B	C
1.	**This solution will benefit:**	2	2	1

  1. few people
  2. some people
  3. half the people
  4. most of the people
  5. everyone

		A	B	C
2.	**Hiring a PR firm would probably solve the problem:**	2	2	2

  1. never
  2. eventually
  3. in good time
  4. soon
  5. immediately

		A	B	C
3.	**The community will see this solution:**	3	3	2

  1. very unfavorably
  2. unfavorably
  3. indifferently
  4. favorably
  5. very favorably

		A	B	C
4.	**Hiring a PR firm would be:**	1	1	2

  1. too expensive for the results
  2. expensive
  3. moderately costly
  4. inexpensive
  5. a great deal

Appendix

Exhibit 5
Solution: Visiting Professors

	Planner	A	B	C
1.	**Faculty attitude toward hiring renowned visiting professors will be:**	4	3	4
	1. antagonistic			
	2. disapproving			
	3. tolerant			
	4. approving			
	5. wildly enthusiastic			
2.	**Hiring renowned visiting professors will be:**	3	2	2
	1. impossible			
	2. extremely difficult			
	3. difficult			
	4. do-able			
	5. easy			
3.	**Community leaders will:**	3	4	2
	1. disapprove			
	2. not care			
	3. be interested			
	4. be supportive			
	5. change their minds about the school			
4.	**Hiring renowned professors will solve the image problem:**	2	3	3
	1. never			
	2. eventually			
	3. in good time			
	4. soon			
	5. immediately			
5.	**This solution will be:**	1	3	3
	1. too expensive for the results			
	2. fairly costly			
	3. only moderately costly			
	4. a pretty good deal			
	5. cheap at any price			

Exhibit 6
Solution: Tougher Admission Standards

Planner	A	B	C
1. **In practice, tough standards would be:**	4	5	3
1. difficult to change			
2. inflexible			
3. somewhat rigid			
4. fairly easy to change			
5. highly flexible			
2. **Tougher standards would probably improve the school's image:**	3	4	4
1. never			
2. someday			
3. in good time			
4. soon			
5. immediately			
3. **This solution would probably reduce enrollment:**	1	2	2
1. like a kick in the head			
2. too much			
3. noticeably			
4. somewhat			
5. not a bit			
4. **Raising standards and the school's mission:**	4	5	5
1. are polar opposites			
2. seem inconsistent			
3. match up slightly			
4. are consistent			
5. conform well			

Appendix

Exhibit 7
Solution: Beautify the Campus

	Planner	A	B	C
1.	**Making the campus pretty will solve the problem:**	2	1	1
	1. fat chance			
	2. eventually			
	3. in good time			
	4. soon			
	5 immediately			
2.	**Students, parents, and faculty will applaud the move:**	4	3	4
	1. never			
	2. not much			
	3. indifferently			
	4. sympathetically			
	5. enthusiastically			
3.	**The return on the dollar spent will be:**	4	3	3
	1. a losing deal			
	2. break-even			
	3. moderate			
	4. substantial			
	5. a knock-out			
4.	**Spiffing up the campus will:**	2	3	3
	1. benefit no one			
	2. help a few			
	3. benefit a good many people			
	4. benefit a lot of people			
	5. help everybody			

Planning for Colleges and Universities

Step 6: These solutions figures should be tabulated in the same manner outlined in Step 5.

Solution	Planner	A	B	C	Total	Average
PR Firm						
Question	1	2	2	1	5	1.67
	2	2	2	2	6	2.00
	3	3	3	2	8	2.67
	4	1	1	2	4	<u>1.33</u>
					Total	7.67
Visiting Professors						
Question	1	4	3	4	11	3.67
	2	3	2	2	7	2.33
	3	3	4	2	9	3.00
	4	2	3	3	8	2.67
	5	1	3	3	7	<u>2.33</u>
					Total	14.00
Raise Standards						
Question	1	4	5	3	12	4.00
	2	3	4	4	11	3.67
	3	1	2	2	5	1.67
	4	4	5	5	14	<u>4.67</u>
					Total	14.00
Beautify Campus						
Question	1	2	1	1	4	1.33
	2	4	3	4	11	3.67
	3	4	3	3	10	3.33
	4	2	3	3	8	<u>2.67</u>
					Total	11.00

Appendix

	Total of Averages	Grand Averages
PR Firm	7.67	1.92
Visiting Professors	14.00	2.80
Raise Standards	14.00	3.50
Beautify Campus	11.00	2.75

The preferred solution apparently is raising admission standards followed by hiring renowned visiting professors, beautifying the campus, and hiring a public relations firm. Thus planners, who could not agree before, now have agreed that the central problem facing the college is its poor image in the community and that it can be solved by raising admission standards. [See Coleman for a case study of this solution.] These two pieces of information were produced objectively and systematically. There should be very little rancor carrying over into future discussions, thereby freeing planners to undertake the next phase of the planning cycle.

The Nominal Group Planning Model

Also valuable in reaching a consensus is the Nominal Group Planning Model.[2] It is essentially a process for taking advantage of a diversity of opinions and values in a systeatic way. It is appropriate for:

- problem exploration
- knowledge exploration
- priority development
- program development
- program evaluation

Since the mechanics of the process are about the same for each application, it is probably a good idea, for the sake of comparison with Simplex, to walk through an example of how it can be used to develop priorities.

Step 1: Structure the decision-making group. As with Simplex and most other group decision processes, it is a good idea to decide right at the outset how big the group should be

---

[2] Modified from A.L. Delbecq and Andrew H. Van de Ven, "A Group Process Model for Problem Identification and Program Planning," *Journal of Applied Behavioral Sciences* (July, 1971), pp. 361-376; and Delbecq and Van de Ven, "The Nominal Group as a Research Instrument for Exploratory Health Studies," *American Journal of Public Health* (March, 1972), pp. 337-342.

Appendix

and whether or not it should have subgroups. Mostly this depends on the complexity of the issue. If it is complex and far-reaching, more people should be involved. An example of this would be a school's complete overhaul of its curriculum. This would demand a planning group large enough to represent a cross-section of ideas, personalities, and values. Take care, though, that the group is not too large because it might become a black hole into which everything goes in and nothing ever comes out.

A complex issue might also dictate that various subgroups be set up to handle specialized matters more efficiently. Each subgroup should reach a consensus on its own topic. When subgroup consensus is reached, that information should be brought before the entire planning group. The whole group could then begin its own nominal group process by considering subgroup work plus anything else that comes up. As a general rule, full group results will be much better if subgroups reach their consensuses first. Otherwise, the whole planning effort can be waylaid by an unresolved narrow subtopic.

Step 2: Define the dimensions of the issue. Each participant should be given a form like the one shown as Exhibit 8. This asks everyone to list all the key factors needed to judge the seriousness of a problem. These factors should be both real and imagined and include personal knowledge and experience, colleagues' views, experiences from other schools, and so forth.

If possible, no one should talk while filling out the form; it's too distracting. Also, do not allow anyone, especially the chairman of the planning group, to offer examples of key factors. This might defeat the purpose of the exercise which is to get everyone's unpolluted opinion.

When Exhibit 8 is completed, each participant should also fill out another form, again in silence, similar to Exhibit 9. This asks planners to catalogue all the problems they can think of which hinder their college's fulfilling its mission (presuming that the mission itself is not a problem).

Step 3: When everybody is satisfied that he can think of nothing else to jot down, the group's chairman should either bring forward a large flip chart or, if unavoidable, go to the chalkboard. [A flip chart is really better, though, because it records what ground the committee has already covered. Too, it records a line of thinking which may be valuable for later discussions.] In a round-robin fashion, each planner then offers one factor from his Exhibit 8 list which the chairman records on the flip chart. No one else should talk while this is going on-- again, it's too distracting and interferes with the flow of information. One planner after another must recite a single factor until all of them are recorded. Next, the chairman flips to a new page and repeats the process for identifying perceived problems from Exhibit 9.

Appendix

Exhibit 8

Factors for Determining Problem Seriousness

List the factors important to you for determining how serious is any problem on campus.

1.
2.
3.
4.

Exhibit 9

Problems on Campus

List all the problems you can think of which interfere with reaching the college's mission.

1.
2.
3.
4.

Step 4: After all factors and problems are recorded, the chairman must now lead the group in a discussion of the ideas on the flip chart. The purpose of this is to clarify, elaborate, defend, and dispute listed items. New items may be added at this time; none may be eliminated. Members must judge for themselves if the key factors from the master list fit the problems. If they do, discussion should proceed one item at a time until all of them have been covered to everyone's satisfaction. It is probably a good idea to set a time limit on the discussion or else it may never end.

Step 5: Next, each participant should rank in order the five (or whatever) most important problems he perceives. The most important problem should be ranked "5" and the least important "1". These rankings should then be recorded on the flip chart by the chairman. When that is done, there will be a table showing how every member ranks every important problem. Then the rankings for each problem are summed across to yield a measure of total importance. Exhibit 10 is an example of this tally sheet.

Appendix

Exhibit 10
Tally Sheet for Rankings

Planner

Problems	A	B	C	D	E	Total
Low Faculty Morale	4	4	3	5	1	17
Declining Enrollment	2	3	4	2	3	14
Unattractive Campus	1	1	2	1	2	7
Low Salaries	3	2	1	3	5	14
Poor Community Image	5	5	5	4	4	23

Step 6: After ranking, the chairman should lead everyone in a discussion of the figures. At this point, members should reclarify, elaborate, defend, or dispute these preliminary results. In all likelihood, there will be considerable discussion, even debate, over what the tally shows. This discussion is necessary and important to the process and should be encouraged. So long as individual members concentrate their remarks on ideas and not on their fellow planners ["...you dolt...!], the discussion should flow along without too much heat. By the way, these rankings are ordinal only and do not reflect relative importance very well.

Step 7: For the final step, planners must attach numerical values of importance to the problems. Not all problems, of course, have to be important to all members. They should rank only those which are important to them. Problems which are critically important should receive a value of 100, whereas less

Planning for Colleges and Universities

important problems should receive less, say, 50 or 20 or 10 or even 0. What is vital here is that planners relate a problem's significance to the significance of all other problems. Each problem's values are summed across participants, as is shown in Exhibit 11.

Exhibit 11
Final Rankings Tally Sheet

			Planner			
Problem	A	B	C	D	E	Total
Low Faculty Morale	90	90	60	100	10	350
Declining Enrollment	40	40	50	20	20	170
Unattractive Campus	0	20	40	10	15	85
Low Salaries	60	30	10	50	100	250
Poor Community Image	100	100	80	60	25	36

These cardinal rankings indicate better than those in Exhibit 10 college planners' true beliefs. By giving the largest weighted total to Poor Community Image, they are signalling it as the most important issue. As a consequence, it should be addressed first. It should be accorded highest priority during subsequent group processing of potential solutions. The four remaining issues will have to wait until another time for consideration.

Appendix

The Nominal Group Planning Model can likewise be used for arriving at solutions to stated problems. If poor image is the major problem, planners must attack its solution in exactly the same way they learned it was the biggest problem. All seven steps need to be repeated, ending up this time with a weighted total of possible solutions. The one with the largest total should be implemented since it is the most attractive.

ABOUT THE AUTHORS

Stephen D. Hogan, Ph.D., is a Visiting Professor of Finance at the University of Tennessee. He has devoted much of his academic career to assisting large and small educational institutions in their planning endeavors. He has also worked in the private and public sectors at the national level to develop operational and strategic plans. Dr. Hogan is a member of the Society for College and University Planning.

Harold E. Knight, III, M.H.A. has been a management consultant for 17 years. He is currently President of Washington Consulting & Management Associates, Inc. Mr. Knight has assisted a wide variety of organizations in developing their planning processes and strategic plans. His work has embraced the dynamics of client environments throughout the United States, Latin America and Asia. His hands-on experience and practical suggestions have been particularly helpful to organizations just beginning to formalize their planning activities.